Springing Forward

Gina Harris and Liza Edwards

Hawthorn Press

Published by Hawthorn Press, Hawthorn House, 1 Lansdown Lane, Stroud, Gloucestershire, GL5 1BJ, UK
Tel: (01453) 757040 Fax: (01453) 751138
email: info@hawthornpress.com
Website: www.hawthornpress.com

Illustrations by Viv Quillin
Cover illustration by Viv Quillin
Cover design by Patrick Roe, Southgate Solutions, Stroud, Glos.
Designed by Liza Edwards
Typesetting by Jim Sweeney, Hawthorn Press, Stroud, Glos.
Printed by The Cromwell Press, Trowbridge, Wilts.
Reprinted 2005
Printed on paper sourced from sustained managed forests and elemental chlorine free.

British Library Cataloguing in Publication Data applied for

ISBN 1 869 890 40 X

Contents

For Liz and Jenny
who created Springboard,
cherished, nurtured and guided her,
and set her free to become
a force for good throughout the world

About the Authors

Gina

Gina Harris is a highly-experienced developer of people. A self-employed trainer and facilitator for ten years, Gina was one of the first licensed trainers for the Springboard Programme. She is currently building up a life-coaching practice, together with exploring a new career as a writer. She believes passionately in work-life balance and in everyone realising their full potential.

Gina combines her development work with a peaceful home life in the Peak District, accompanied by her husband, a demanding white cat called Boo, and sometimes one or more of their three adult children.

Liza

Creativity is Liza's hallmark - writing, marketing, designing, playing the piano, singing - anything that involves imagination, ideas and people. Most of all, she loves using her energy to make a positive difference in the world. Her association with Springboard includes working at the head office in a variety of roles, as well as being a participant in the programme.

Liza lives in a small, cosy home with a modern study full of books, a snowboarding other-half and an ageing cocker spaniel called Basil.

Viv

Viv Quillin is a very funny cartoonist whose inspiring humour has illuminated numerous publications ranging from 'New Internationalist' to 'Slimmers'. She is helplessly committed to women's development and has written and cartooned eight books of her own humour, including the best selling 'Opposite Sex' which tramped sensitively through women's sexuality.

She also loves illustrating other people's books and articles, mostly with their permission.

Working in a red painted studio with a tasteful fake tiger skin pelmet, she's currently launching her own range of greetings cards.

Thanks

Joint thanks

Hawthorn Press –especially Anne, Martin, Rachel and Frances
Jenny and Liz
Springboard Network worldwide
Springboard participants

Gina

I know that without the interest and enthusiasm of Liza, this book would never have been written. It's many years since I first suggested that there was a book within the worldwide Springboard community waiting to be produced. Naturally, it was then expected that I would take on this mighty task. After much research and prevarication, it was thanks to Liza's involvement that the whole thing took off. Thanks, Liza, for keeping my nose to the grindstone and your ear to the ground, and both of our shoulders to the wheel (or keyboard, as it's called these days).

Thanks to Mick, for his love and support, to Liz and Jenny, without whom none of this would have happened, and to Gail, who saves me from having to do any housework – bliss!

Gina P Harris

Liza

My first thanks to Gina – ever since I knew what it meant, I longed to be 'an author', but never imagined it would be so enjoyable. Because of our differing backgrounds and perspectives, and especially because of our different characters, writing with you has been a real development experience in its own right. I know that others share my warm thoughts of you as a treasured and much-loved friend, but I am proud to call you my 'co-author' as well.

Another overwhelming thank you to Scott Davis, the man I share my life with. Even though you may not always understand my reasoning on certain passions, you have always supported me, encouraged me and told me 'get on with it' when I needed the boost! Your belief in me has often outweighed my own, and your positive view of the world has always inspired me.

Family thanks are to my mom, dad and brothers who always encouraged me to write, be creative and soar high, plus my in-law family, for your much-appreciated support and pride in this 'adopted' daughter. Finally, a personal thank you to Jenny and Liz, Nicola and Celia, who, aside from being great colleagues, gave me inspiration, a reason to laugh, and encouragement to be 'an oasis of calm' in any situation!

Foreword

Having left school at 16 and worked in my local Boots Chemist for two years, I felt there had to be more to life than I was experiencing and more to me than was being demanded.

If you feel like that – and your age is irrelevant – 'Springing Forward' could be helpful in clearing the tangled undergrowth that's stopping you exploring an ambition, an idea, a dream or a passion.

We are not Sleeping Beauties, we're women, capable of being and doing anything and everything we want to. But wanting alone won't achieve – work plus determination, curiosity and courage probably will. And every woman I've ever known has that, plus a great deal more.

So go for it – say 'Yes' first, and worry after. Change your life, your community, the world. Spring Forward!

Best wishes,

Glenda Jackson, MP

About the Notebook

Throughout 'Springing Forward', you'll notice a series of *Notebook* sections. Although this isn't a workbook, experience shows that writing your thoughts, hopes and aspirations can really help your development.

It's entirely your choice, but using a notebook will bring out the best of the ideas in this book.

Why not take the time to choose yourself a really special notebook to write in, and make it the first step in committing to making the most of you?

Chapter One
Whatever You Want

'I wanted to change the direction in which my life was going but I felt indecisive and frightened of change. However, in order to change direction, there were things I both wanted and needed to change about myself.'

Claire, UK

What changes do you dream of making?
If you could have anything, what would it be?
When was the last time you made a wish-list, even just in your mind?

If it weren't natural to want more for yourself, there would never be any progress, evolution, or development – but changes rarely happen automatically. They usually require some effort.

Whenever you have a dream or an ambition, it means you want something to change. Let this be the start of positive changes for you, for your future.

Healthy Selfishness

The hardest thing for many of us is even to admit that we want things. Each of us has a different view of dreaming and wanting, but many of us feel that it is wrong or 'selfish' to want things for ourselves.

There is such a thing as healthy selfishness – and that is, simply, being the person or self we really want to be.

Why is this good? Because if we spend all our time being 'unselfish', we are likely to become drained, exhausted and even resentful. If we believe the truth of "Love your neighbour as yourself", we must accept that we need to "love ourselves" first.

NOTEBOOK

YOUR WISHLIST

In your notebook, write down your wish-list. You may have done something like this before, or this may be the first time you have ever thought about it – but whichever it is, write down anything that comes to mind.

Try not to think about it too much, and don't exclude anything just because you think, "That's impossible." Writing down what you really want is a powerful way of getting things into perspective and committing yourself to future action.

Whatever You Want

It's time to think about what you want – not just material things, but what you would want if you could change anything. It's about you, your own ideas, and nobody is going to challenge you about any of it, so let your imagination go wild!

Think about:

- Yourself: who you are, how you feel about yourself, your personality

- Your situation: where you are now in your life, where you'd like to be

- Material items: things that would make a difference to you if you owned them

- Activities: things that you would like to try or achieve

Some positive effects of thinking about your hopes and dreams include:

- You are recharging your batteries and building up energy

- You have something to look forward to and a focus for the future

- You are encouraging creative thought, and expanding your imagination

- You are more likely to take action on something you've become excited about.

My wishbook is steadily filling up, and I have already started to 'grant' myself some wishes, such as my trip to Italy and tickets to concerts. As well as things that cost money, the wishbook contains things that are cheap to do – such as having flowers in my house - so I can always concentrate on the low-budget wishes when money is tight!

Anne, UK

Having my goals written down helped to keep me really focused.

Pauline, Australia

'I would love to' versus 'I can't, because...'

Often, when we are thinking of what we want, we think first about the barriers – money, a disability, lack of transport or where we live. If there are factors that you can't change, bear them in mind but still think creatively, beyond the boundaries.

Focus on the dream. Think back to your childhood and remember what you used to dream of becoming and doing.

Did you ever say, 'When I grow up, I'm going to be...'? Perhaps you were certain you'd be a pop star, a deep-sea-diver, a vet?

Here you are, at the grown-up age you used to dream about, and perhaps you've stopped dreaming.

The reality of growing up is that we take on adult responsibilities and the everyday is usually more about what we feel we <u>have</u> to do, and less about what we actually <u>want</u> to do.

It's time to allow yourself some of that healthy selfishness.

How often have you felt like spending the day doing one thing, but ended up doing another because you felt you 'should'?

How often have you said with a sigh, 'I suppose I ought to...'?

Hardening of the Oughteries: symptoms and cures

When we do pause to think about our real wishes and aims, we often find we're so boxed in by 'I should..' and 'I ought to..', that 'I'd love to..' rarely gets a look in. It's an infectious disease known as The Hardening of the Oughteries!

> *As soon as you hear yourself saying*
> *'ought to' or 'should', beware!*
> *These are other people's voices and not your own.*

One of the by-products of this disease is an underlying feeling of anger. This anger is connected with being powerless to lead our lives as we would really like to.

Many of us have been brought up not to express or even acknowledge anger. We find it hard to be angry with the people we love even though it is often because of them and their demands on us that our lives feel so constrained. As a result, we suppress our anger, and it can build up, year after year, sometimes causing physical and mental problems.

If you feel that you don't have the time to be 'you', it's only natural that you might feel angry about it – and then even guilty about the anger. This way we can find ourselves in a vicious circle of bad feeling, even if many of us don't stop to recognise it.

The cure for this disease is to find a way to break the circle.

This doesn't mean abandoning all your responsibilities, but it's only fair to allow your own desires as much 'air time' as you give to the desires of others.

PERFECT DAY

Imagine that all you had to think about for the next day was you. No-one else's views or preferences to take into account. You have a whole day in which you can do what you want, go where you want, act how you want – let's even say that money is no object.

What would you do?

Think about this for a few minutes and make some notes in your book. Just jot down whatever comes into your head. The heading might be 'My Perfect Day'.
On the opposite page, write down how you would spend a normal day. Compare the two days.

What is the difference? Where are the gaps? How often do you do any of the items on your perfect day?

By comparing your Perfect Day with your Real Day, you may been surprised to discover how much of your life is spent in ways you may not have chosen. If you could bring even a little of your perfect day into your every-day, you'd be getting closer to the life you really want for yourself.

> **"** *Finally, I realised that spending time for yourself is not a crime.* **"**

Kamla Sharma, India

Having the time of your life

There is one commodity that is limited for all of us – time. Many of us go from one routine to the next, without reminding ourselves of how precious time is and how little of it we may have. However, it is also the one thing that we all have some control over – we all have some choice about how we spend our time.

For a woman, it often seems difficult to remember – or even to discover for the first time – how to want things for herself. Women tend to feel 'better' if they want things for others – for their partners, children, friends or colleagues.

The Office for National Statistics commissioned a survey on how men and women of all ages spend their time (Time Use Survey, 1995). Whether in full-time or part-time employment, women were found to spend over twice as much time as men on 'housework, cooking and shopping', and in both cases, the women had less 'free time' to themselves each week.

Does this sound familiar?

Coming up to the new millennium, I realised that when I was a kid, I had had all these plans for what I would be doing by the year 2000. And I realised that I had stopped dreaming like I used to when I was a child, or even a teenager, and my days as an adult were spent in routine.

I had got myself into a rut of going to work to get the money to pay the bills and maybe get 'decent' presents for others at Christmas. My younger self would have been amazed at how boring I'd become. Another thing I realised – I only wanted what I knew I could have, so that I could tell myself it felt like a treat when actually it wasn't.

So, I looked at myself afresh. Okay, I wasn't going to be a pop star, but I joined the Choral Society; and I still have to go to work to pay the bills, but I also treat myself once in a while.

Sophie, UK

Why not?

Now that you have spent time thinking seriously about all the things that you might want, all the things that you would change if you could, there is a hard question to face: why not?

Why can't you do all these things and more? What's to stop you?

In spite of all the other constraints in your life, the main barrier between you and what you really want is your own self, every time.

Now that you have dared to dream about what you want, it's time to look at who this person is that wants these things. You need to devote a little time to gain an awareness of why you have these goals, what is important to you, what might stop you and how you feel about the path ahead. This is the starting point.

Why do you want this?

Know what you want, be prepared to take risks, and value each step in the right direction – however small.

Gillian, Australia

The first step from where you are now to where you want to be is to gain a sound awareness of your self. This means looking at who you are, what your situation is, and most importantly of all, why you want things to change.

Your motivation, what drives you towards something, can be negative or positive. Before you start working towards a goal, be honest with yourself as to why you want to have this or achieve that.

Negative motivations:
Negative motivations mostly relate to other people rather than to ourselves.

This might include:
- 'because it will show them I can'
- 'because they expect me to'
- 'because I said I would'
- 'because I'll look foolish if I don't'
- 'because I feel I ought to'
- 'because everyone else has got one'

If you feel that you must do or have something because of guilt, jealousy, obligation or competition, it is a false start. Make them your own dreams for your own reasons.

Positive motivations:
As you might imagine, positive motivations come primarily from *you*.

This might include:
- 'because I have always wanted to'
- 'because I want to change for the better'
- 'because I want to do this just for me'
- 'because I just feel I need to'
- 'because I want to make the most of myself and this life'
- 'because it's a dream'
- 'because I can'
- 'because I just don't know if I can'

Some motivations that involve other people's wishes can be positive, but *you* need to feel them from the heart as well. Do it because you want to.

What is important to you?

Quite simply, what do you value and how much?

Values are not necessarily about your beliefs. They are what you feel is important in life, and how strongly you feel about something.

For example, an ecological value of always buying recycled paper may be more important to you than cost. You might value your new car each year, and choose to work overtime in order to save for that.

What are the real motivators for you in your life?

If you can identify what is important to you, what excites you and what you hold dear, you have recognised your values. Some will be principles or standards, some may be deep feelings.

Whatever your 'package' of values, yours is unique. Some will be inherited, some have come to you through your life experiences.

I felt trapped and was looking for another job when I found out I was pregnant.

I didn't feel it was ethical to take up a new job without mentioning that I was pregnant, but as I didn't think anyone would hire me if I did tell them, I decided to stay put.

Be true to your beliefs and values even when you're surrounded by negative pressures.

Zoe, Australia

People are usually happiest when they live according to their own values, rather than someone else's.

Take a moment to think about what matters to you, and how this colours your life and the choices you make.

Your values may include:

- love of family, children and home
- co-operation and finding agreements
- making a positive difference
- getting and giving support and encouragement
- making and maintaining deep and lasting friendships
- a longing for everyone to have enough – time, space, food, work and leisure
- a need to express creativity in a wide variety of ways
- a balance between work and home
- an overriding belief that people are more important than possessions or money

I knew that my family was the most important thing in my life, especially while my children were little, but my actions didn't seem to correspond to that value. I had been working in a big company for 10 years and my work meant me taking time away from my children – overtime, travelling, tiredness and so on.

I wrote down some things about my life, like how old I was, how many working years I had ahead of me, and how short a time my girls would need me. I became sure that I was not doing what I wanted and what I needed for a balanced life.

Pia, Finland

What will stop me?

Often, we decide consciously or unconsciously that we shouldn't have or do something, because of other people. It might be that we are worried someone else won't like it, or that they will be jealous, or that someone will laugh at us or judge us.

These feelings stem from fear, lack of confidence or self-esteem, lack of belief in our own vision and intuition. For these and other reasons, many of us end up not doing or having things that are really important to us.

> *It is better to regret something that you have done than something you didn't do.*

Know your enemy!

As this is to be the first step towards whatever you really want, it's worth spending some time looking at what might hinder your progress.

This is a positive move. If you look at the likely difficulties now, you will be laying sound foundations to build on. By thinking ahead about any hindrances early on, they can't catch you unawares.

NOTEBOOK

REASON – OR EXCUSE?

Make a list in your notebook of what is stopping you making changes in your life. Include everything you can think of, big and small, important and trivial.

Now look at your list critically and put beside each an R or an E.

R is for Reason and E is for Excuse.

Reason = sensible conduct, what is right or practical
Excuse = an attempt to lessen the blame

Only you can decide honestly whether your list has more Es than Rs, or whether some of your Rs should really be Es!

Your list will reveal if you are using someone or something outside you as an excuse not to go for a dream, perhaps because it is easier than the risk of not achieving what you really want.

" *I know that life isn't always wonderful, but we all have the power within us to make our own decisions, and to make changes if we aren't happy with things. One of my greatest realisations is that the happiness is a journey,* **"** *not a destination.*

Donna-Marie, Australia

What can I do about it?

Awareness, commitment and honesty: it all comes down to you.

You need to have a real understanding of where you are now, before you can start on the journey to where you want to be.

It's also important that you are committed to whatever you are undertaking, even if it seems to be a small goal. When you have strong beliefs in what you are doing, and you have a clear idea of how it fits in with your life, then you stand the best chance of succeeding.

Yes, there is such a thing as the perfect moment to take the first step towards your dreams.

That moment is right now, because you may never get another chance as good as this in all your life.

In your heart, you know this is true – and anything that stops you is little more than an excuse.

Ellie, UK

Chapter Two
This Is Your Life

*'The world's attitudes and the rules that surround us could be a heavy
burden, but they can also yield surprising possibilities, leading us to
different experiences and new points of view.'*

Pirkko, Finland

Perhaps you are beginning to get a clearer picture of where you want
to be, and what changes you want to make. Now's the time to look at
how you fit in with the bigger picture.

Only by being more aware of the world and your place within it can
you decide what you are happy with, and what you are not.

How did you get to be you?

Whoever you are comes from two main sources: your own life and character ('biography') and the greater life of the world that you live in ('history').

Biography

Biography is important because it is your unique experience – two people raised in the same environment can have a completely different outlook on life, and can end up with very different experiences.

Your biography is your personal history, and depends not only on external circumstances, but also on your individual character.

NOTEBOOK

YOU AND YOUR 'BIOGRAPHY'

- Which events in your life do you think have affected you a lot?

- Which people in your life have had a major influence on you?

- Which experiences do you feel alienate you from other people?

- Which experiences give you something in common with other people?

History

History is what lies beyond you and came before you. It provided the backdrop for all your experiences. History can relate to traditions, culture, religion, even national or global events.

If you had been born a man rather than a woman, or in a different country or time, your experiences might have been dramatically different.

"

In India, women's progress up the ladder is constrained by the assumption that they will be the main child-carers. Having been brought up in the patriarchal tradition, most women are unable to see themselves as being successful in their careers without compromising their family-defined roles of wife, mother and caregiver. **"**

Radha Swaminathan, Indian Springboard Trainer

NOTEBOOK

YOU AND YOUR 'HISTORY'

- What aspects of history do you think make it difficult for you to achieve what you want?

- What aspects of history make it easier to achieve what you want?

Why is this outside world so important?

None of us lives in isolation. The outside world, with its constraints, barriers and opportunities, provides you with the framework for <u>your</u> life, no matter how individual you are. The issues that surround you will affect what you want to do and how you move towards your goals, dreams and ambitions.

Your immediate world consists of your current situation, cultural or religious experiences, even the circle of people that you come into contact with every day. Many of us find that some things, such as the friends who are closest to us, will change as we go through stages of life, whilst others remain constant, such as our family members.

The immediate world is the one on which we can have the most effect. We are more likely to be able to change these circumstances quickly if we want to – such as redecorating the bedroom or meeting new people.

NOTEBOOK

YOU AND YOUR WORLD

- What do you like about your immediate world?

- What, if anything, would you change?

Being a woman

Even in this new millennium, it seems that for some women little has changed. On the one hand, women have access to education, can get a degree, and can even get to managerial levels in organisations, but whilst it is an improvement on the beginning of the 1900s, we still do not have equality.

66

While the position of men and women has changed dramatically since the EOC was set up in 1975, it is hugely frustrating that many of the fundamental barriers to true sex equality still remain. 99

Julie Mellor,
Chair of the Equal Opportunities Commission

I never stopped to think about the fact that I was female until I started to work for a living. I was at managerial level but was still expected to be the coffee waitress – and the only other person expected to perform that role was the (female) receptionist. Not one of the men was ever expected to, regardless of their seniority.

Until experiencing that, I had thought I'd succeed or fail on my own merits, not because of being female. I couldn't believe that such sexist attitudes still existed in the 1990s.

Lisa, UK

Miss, Mrs or Ms?

*'Lord, how ashamed I should be of not being married
before three and twenty!'*

Lydia, in Jane Austen's Pride and Prejudice (1813)

In Jane Austen's time, a woman was dependent on her male relatives for money, shelter and sustenance – if she were not married by the time her father died, a woman had very limited options for supporting herself or her family.

In the 21st Century, in many parts of the world, we have more choices and far more independence. Indeed, an increasing number of women choose to live on their own. However, there is still an expectation in most societies that women should reveal their marital status while men are simply 'Mr'.

The average age for getting married and the average age for becoming a mother have been rising over the years whilst women make the most of their independence.

Couples are no longer under such pressure to be married. In many countries, a couple can live together without being married, and can have children together without suffering general condemnation as they would have done even thirty years ago.

Where do we get our view of 'who we ought to be'?

Expectations, standards, impossible role models and a glossy image of the ideal woman are around us every day. These images are so much part of our culture that we hardly notice their intrusion.

Spend one afternoon or evening looking carefully at the advertisements and the news, and you will see where many of our less realistic aspirations come from. There seems to be an ideal for your car, butter, furniture, even a colour of the season that we should all be wearing.

There are expectations on all of us, but those for women have always been more demanding. It is important to remind yourself that you still have the freedom to choose how you respond.

I remember someone saying to me that if I was ever planning to become a mother, I had better be prepared for the guilt.

If I went to work, I would feel guilty about not spending time with my kids. If I stayed at home, I would feel guilty because I 'ought' to be capable of working as well. The release came when I realised that all I had to worry about was what felt right for me and for my family.

Maureen, Ireland

What labels do you live with?

Take a moment to circle some of the words below and add some of your own 'labels' in the space provided.

These are words that are used to describe and define you.

Everybody forms an opinion of you – whether you want them to or not.

Mandy, Australia

I AM

Woman	Asian	teenage	Man	Australian
child	disabled	fat	British	middle-aged	thin
Black	Chinese	Mother	European	daughter
White	partner	short	young	tall	old
wife	Finnish	Indian	Secretary	manager

You can spend a large proportion of your life concerned with what other people think of you. This can be a tremendous waste of energy as you will never know exactly what they really think.

Judge your successes and merits by your own standards. To be fair, leave other people to live by their standards, not yours.

Thinking without the labels

Everyone is unique. Whilst we can be described in terms of 'labels' – our appearance, race, age, nationality, gender – these are only small items. Each of us has the potential to grow way beyond any pigeonhole or boundary that can be used to describe us.

> *Labels are how the outside world sometimes sees you – they should never dictate how you see yourself.*

Think of yourself as one unique package, with perhaps the single label of your name or nickname. The person you are, regardless of what you own, do or look like, is all that counts.

Who is the real you?

We all have different sides of ourselves that come to the fore in different situations, and this is a great part of the human ability to adapt.

The character that you portray when you are at work or in a professional, serious environment may be very different from the person you are at home, or with your friends or family.

You might feel that you play many roles. You might be daughter, manager, sister, mother, partner, wife, friend – all in one day!

It is important that you have a sense of who <u>you</u> are, beyond any of the roles that you play.

NOTEBOOK

ROLES

- When you are alone, do you feel exhausted by the different roles or characters that you present to the outside world?

- When you have quiet time to yourself, do you feel you know the 'real you'?

How might things be different?

Daring to dream and to want things for yourself can take a certain amount of courage and conviction.

The best tool you can have to help towards your success in any goal or endeavour is belief in your self. It is possible to be diplomatic and likeable whilst also being confident and proud of who you are.

However you think the world sees you, always focus on how you feel about yourself. Once you feel comfortable with yourself, you can look at the outside world in a whole new light.

Jennifer Davies, BBC

At the beginning of 1989 I had been a Studio Manager with BBC World Service for 11 years. I'd completed a number of attachments to other departments and everyone else seemed to be expecting me to move on in my career but I was uncertain about my path; I felt I was stuck in a rut – people were saying to me "Are you still only a Studio Manager?"

I jumped at the opportunity to take part in the first Springboard Programme, hoping it would help me to put things into perspective and decide what I wanted to do. It certainly did that and more! It opened up a whole new area of opportunity and gave me the confidence to "go for it".

One of the most important aspects of the programme was its "holistic" attitude, concentrating as it does not on career development but on personal development. By working through the workbook, I realised what was important to me as a person as well as analysing my strengths and weaknesses and assessing what I wanted from my career.

At the end of the Programme I knew why I enjoyed being a Studio Manager and why I found production rewarding but very stressful. I no longer felt that I was still a Studio Manager just because I hadn't managed to move on. I recognised that I was proud of my experience and ability in my chosen field.

At the beginning of 1990 I won promotion to a position as Assistant Shift Leader with responsibility for more junior colleagues – a role that I had long believed I was well-qualified to fulfil but had not had the self-confidence to compete for.

Jennifer says that she already believed she could handle the role with greater responsibility, but she lacked the self-confidence to compete for it. Sometimes, even when we have got to the stage of recognising our own abilities and know what our goal is, we do not have the confidence to make it happen.

By asking herself honest questions about goals and priorities, Jennifer was able to identify her <u>own</u> goals and work towards them. Progressing along the usual route wouldn't have suited her, and once she had thought about her own strengths and gained her confidence, she found the right path for her and moved on.

The right path is the right path for <u>you</u>, not necessarily the route that everyone else seems to be taking.

Changing things for the future

We are all moulded by our environment, but when we are restricted, suffocated or pressured by it, our ability to think clearly or positively may be affected. If we can learn from our past, rather than be oppressed by it, the future will be brighter.

If your parents had unreasonable expectations of you, you may be more sensitive to how you treat your own children, or other people.

If you know that you have spent your life unhappy with how you look, think about where the 'ideal' came from – then you can decide whether you <u>choose</u> this as your ideal, or if you have a completely different view.

In a world without praise or blame, who would you be?

Beyond the box

Instead of seeing what others see, and instead of seeing the barriers, the expectations and the stereotypes, look beyond the box.

The great changes and developments that have happened in history did not come about by people focusing on why something wasn't possible. They came about because a few people saw beyond the boundaries or the 'norm' and believed that they could do something different.

First, see how things are, and if you don't like something, look at what you can do to change it.

Biography and history provide the setting but you make the future.

66 *Often we walk around as if we have our heads in a drainpipe, not looking to either side but only seeing the light in the far distance.*

Taking your head out of the drainpipe enables us to see far and wide. **99**

Christine Baines, Springboard Trainer, UK

Chapter Three
Changing Your Inlook

'It's never too late to be what you might have been.'

George Eliot

Time and again through history, people have individually or collectively thought that they knew the limits of their capability, and time and again they have proved themselves wrong. Not long ago, people would have laughed at the idea of men walking on the moon, of a woman Prime Minister in the UK, or a black president in South Africa.

In order to achieve something, you need to believe it is possible. All too often, we concentrate on the barriers, why something is difficult. What we really need is to focus on is how we <u>can</u> make it happen.

What's your 'inlook'?

How you view the world outside is your 'outlook'. To describe how you view your inner self, we have chosen the word 'inlook'. Your belief in yourself and what you are capable of starts from within. If you're constantly putting yourself down or mistrusting your own abilities, it's time for a major internal shift.

A great deal of our conditioning persuades us to think that happiness and fulfilment are things that we get from outside. We aren't often encouraged to look within ourselves and to tap our inner resources. Consider the question, "What makes me happy?" Straight away we give ourselves the impression that happiness is something that is 'done to us'.

As a result, we lose the ability to trust ourselves. The outside world is full of 'experts' who know best what we 'ought' to do in order to be happy. In fact, we are the experts on our own happiness. It's just that we've forgotten, or never learnt, how to listen to our own positive voice.

How often have you said to yourself....?

"   **I'd love to do that, but I just haven't got the time.**   **"**

Pause for a moment to listen to some of the voices that you do hear. This is the time to be honest about the barriers that you place in front of yourself, and resolve them. Change the way you think, and you can change your world.

There will be the same number of hours in a day tomorrow, or next year. How many of these hours will you spend doing something practical towards your dream?

- **"I've always wanted to try that, but it isn't really me."**

  If it isn't 'you', how come you are the one who has had the idea? And where did you get this fixed idea of 'you'? Why not change it?

- **"I'd love to do that if the kids were older/if I hadn't got children."**

  Of course children are a responsibility, but they are not a full-time job, particularly when they are at school. How will you make the most of the time you have?

- **"I've always wanted to try that, but my partner/friend/family thinks it's a daft idea."**

  What other people think cannot take away from how much something means to you. Don't let other people be the sole reason for you not taking action on a dream or ambition. Their feelings and opinions may be important to you, but it's your life, not theirs.

- **"I'd love to do that but I can't because of my work."**

  Does this mean that if your work situation changed, nothing would stop you? If so, maybe it's time to look at how you can change your work situation. That may become your first goal.

- **"I can't do anything about it right now, but I'll do it after Christmas/next year/when the kids go back to school/when I'm on more money."**

  Putting off a decision or action is as good as saying you'll never get around to it. Most of us know from experience that there is always something else to be done, another reason to put it off a while longer. What difference would it really make to start now?

NOTEBOOK

ADVISE YOURSELF!

Write down the reasons you have <u>now</u> for
not taking action on your goals.

Then write down what you would say if a friend were
offering these as reasons for not
following her dreams.

Imagine someone giving the same advice to you.
How do you react?

Some people seem to have a naturally strong belief in their ability to succeed – and they are often the people who, if they fail, will pick themselves up and try again, or try something new.

**Don't be afraid of 'what might happen'
– be excited about it!**

What are you worth?

When we discover the real potential within ourselves, we bother less and less about the limitations that the outside world tries to put on us. We discover self-esteem – how we really value ourselves – and self-confidence – how we present ourselves to others.

Self-esteem involves finding out what you love and what you enjoy doing, and providing yourself with these things, rather than waiting for someone else to offer them. Caring for yourself is the beginning of self-esteem.

You are valuable because you value yourself. That's enough.

NOTEBOOK

TOP TENS

- List 10 things about yourself that you like – qualities, physical aspects, things you've done.

- List 10 nice things that you could do for yourself (without breaking the bank!).

- Write down in your diary when you are going to do at least four of these in the next two weeks.

Self-confidence

Gaining self-confidence involves facing challenges and difficulties with the reassuring knowledge that you will be able to cope.

Being 'sure of myself' isn't bravado or bragging – it's the solid centre from which you begin to fulfil your potential. It means learning from your mistakes and moving forward.

"
Are you just a passenger on the bus that is your life, or are you in the driving seat? Being a passenger is an easy ride, but being the driver means even if you do take a few wrong turns, at least you choose the route. **"**

Christine Baines, Springboard Trainer, UK

Listen to yourself

When you feel hungry, how do you know what to eat? You listen to your body and decide to go for the toast and honey or the pickled onion straight out of the jar or the crisp, juicy apple.

Just as we know what our body needs if we listen to it, so we can discover what our inner self needs – but we have to make time to listen and we have to be patient.

True self-confidence comes from knowing that you are unique and that no-one else has exactly your combination of qualities and skills. If you don't yet know how to make the most of these, listen to yourself and you'll find out.

Nobody else can live the life that you're meant to lead.

" *A few times in my life I have done things that I instantly felt very strongly for, and it has always turned out to be the right thing for me to do. So I'm learning more and more to trust my intuition.* **"**

Gudrun Lindberg, Swedish Springboard Trainer

Who's responsible for you?

A peculiarly female predicament seems to be that we are fine being responsible for the whole world and its dog, but if we realise that we are actually responsible for ourselves, and for our own future, that suddenly becomes difficult!

It is crucial to recognise and then accept that each of us is responsible for ourselves. We cannot be responsible for another's actions or feelings, even though we may feel that we are.

> *Be prepared to go out there and find your own opportunities, because the right ones won't necessarily find you on their own.*
>
> Zoe, Australia

The only person responsible for where you are, what you do, and what you want is you.

Accepting responsibility for your own life is positive and rewarding – but it's a great challenge. You also have to accept there is no-one to blame for your choices.

Rather than just reacting to what happens around you, make the decision to take charge and make some positive choices.

No-one is better equipped to make choices about your life than you are.

" *Don't wait for the light at the end of the tunnel – run down there and light it yourself!* **"**

Michelle Moynihan, Australian Springboard trainer

From preparation to action

The best way to learn something new or to make a change is to travel gradually from the known to the unknown, the familiar to the unfamiliar.

Through looking at yourself, and looking at your world, you have laid some great groundwork: you know a lot about your situation. If you also build up your confidence and self-esteem, you have the necessary tools to really get going.

When we want to achieve something, the human tendency is either to be so concerned about the whole idea that we never get around to it, or – conversely – to be so excited that we leap ahead without looking.

There is a crucial combination that will maximise your chances of success: preparation and action.

Taking action is all about making it happen for you, bringing your own circumstances closer to your ideal.

When you look back, your path may have been very different from the one you initially envisaged, but that does not matter at all. What matters is that you made a positive decision and started the process.

> *Life is about living, doing, enjoying, trying,*
> *daring, making it happen:*
> *anything less is just existing.*

One step at a time

When you focus on what you really want, it can be overwhelming – 'It's too much' or 'I'll never manage that!' may spring to mind.

You need to see the big picture, but also remember that even the biggest palaces in the world are made up of individual bricks, built upon a sound foundation.

NOTEBOOK

BIT BY BIT

Think for a moment about what you hope to achieve - your dream or goal.

Now note down what your very first step would be – however small – towards this goal.

Put a date by which you want to have made that first step. Also note today's date.

Make that your priority until you can take the next step.

By these small bricks, we build our palaces.

'If I had thought of what I was trying to achieve, I would never have kept going. When I was doing my degree, all I was thinking of was: I need to get this essay done by Friday, and this reading finished by next week. That way, I could take each day with its own priorities, and not get overwhelmed. Next thing I knew, finals were over, and it was time to break open the champagne!'

Arti, UK

Daydreamer or Doer?

Ideas and dreams are beautiful but distant.
Make a decision.
Turn dreams into action.
See the first step and take it.
All the rest will follow.

Karin Blauensteiner, Austrian Springboard Trainer

It might be an unusual thing to say, but I do consider myself a successful woman, at least as far as business is concerned. Sometimes I wonder how I do not seem to fail very often, and I have realised that:

I have a certain place or goal where I want to be. It takes me a long time to figure out what it is that I want, but once I have decided, I go for it.

I always spend time looking at the 'what-ifs'. These are useful to think about, as I then work hard to avoid them or to learn how to deal with them if they do arise. So, I always prepare well, and that gives me the confidence and sense of security that I need.

Never do I think of actually failing. What I do instead is to picture myself doing whatever it is that I am hoping to achieve, and that I am doing it perfectly well. That gives me a lot of ideas, and because it's fun it makes me feel more positive, too.

What else do I need?

You may have thought that you would wait until you had something, knew something, met someone, but these are all ways of putting off what you actually want to start as soon as possible.

When you have a great idea, or a goal that you have dreamt of for a long time, it becomes so bright that you almost fear to approach it. Instead, think of it the other way around – it is so great that you can't wait to get started!

You have got everything you need – all you have to do is make the decision to go for it.

Now you are on your way.

NOTEBOOK

HOLD THAT FEELING

What goal do you have in mind?

Imagine you are already there – how does it feel?

Hold on to that feeling, of achieving your dream and knowing that you've done it.

Whenever you need inspiration or support, or when you find you are thinking negatively and have stopped believing you can 'make it', bring yourself back to that feeling.

Change your inlook, make it happen

Changing your inlook requires you to shift your focus away from the barriers and onto the end-result. This means believing in yourself, cultivating your self-esteem and self-confidence, and making some active decisions.

- Instead of 'I can't, because..', think 'How soon can I make a start?'

- Instead of daydreaming, make it happen

- Instead of complaining, make a positive choice

- Instead of leaving it to other people, accept responsibility for your own life, and enjoy the empowering effects of your own decisions

If you keep 'putting it off until tomorrow', you finally run out of tomorrows.

Today, on the other hand, is right here in front of you.

If a woman is sufficiently ambitious, determined and gifted – there is practically nothing she can't do.

Helen, New Zealand

Chapter Four
Positively People

'Be open to what you can learn from others, and strive to know yourself beyond what you see reflected back from those around you. Recognise and value the people who help you along the way.'

Kerryn, Australia

How many people do you know?

How many people have you met or come into contact with through your lifetime so far?

Contact with other people is tremendously important for all of us. Humans are sociable animals. Whether it's contact with family, friends, colleagues or indirect contact through books, hearsay or other media, people will play an enormous part in your life, and in you getting to where you want to be.

Your relationships with others

Your relationships with other people - from the fleeting conversation with someone you hardly know through to a lifetime friendship - can influence your feelings, decisions and actions enormously.

NOTEBOOK

A PEOPLE PICTURE

- Who do you spend your time with?
- Are they people you're glad to know?
- How do you choose your friends - or do they choose you?
- How do you relate to your family?
- What are you getting out of, and putting in to, your relationships with others?
- Are you making the most of the people in your life, from both your and their points of view?

Family

It is a fact of life – and no, it isn't necessarily fair – that some people are blessed with a wonderful family and others are not. If you have supportive and loving relatives, nurture and value them. Try not to take them for granted or make too many demands on them, but count them as your first and most precious network.

If, on the other hand, you can only expect minimal support from your relatives, concentrate on building up your contacts in other areas. Not having family support is sad but need not be a permanent disadvantage if you actively replace it with good and loyal friends.

In a matter of twelve months, I started a new job, began a course in mechanical drafting and became pregnant. All without much support from my partner. When Krystal was one, we left him and moved in with my Mother.

Through all this I have had support from my Mother, who always encouraged me to try anything.

Janette, Australia

My own childhood was far from ideal and affected my confidence tremendously. This meant that when I became a mum, a loving family environment was all the more precious.

Margaret, UK

Friends

"Oh I get by with a little help from my friends."

Fortunately, you can choose your friends. So do you choose wisely?

Some friends you may have had since childhood and shared so much with that nothing is likely to part you. Other friends will be more recently acquired, some almost without your intention.

Having a small number of really good friends on whom we can rely, through thick and thin, is not something we can leave to chance. Friendship needs time, space, understanding and perseverance.

Investing in friends that you've outgrown or who drain your energy is simply not worth it. In terms of your own development, your time and energy are best spent wisely on the people who really matter to you.

Lesley-Anne, UK

I attended one of the first Springboard programmes in 1991, whilst heavily pregnant with my third son. On the course, I talked for the first time in years about my long-held wish to train as a barrister. One of the women simply said, 'Well, why don't you do it then?'- so I did.

In October 1995, I was finally called to the Bar. It was the most fantastic feeling to have made it! I'm not sure that I would have achieved any of this without that initial support and inspiration from other women, and I'd like to offer the same encouragement to others.

"   *If I find myself around people who make me feel bad, I don't hang around.*   **"**

Sue, Australia

People at work – colleagues and managers

It's common knowledge that the majority of jobs in organisations are now filled internally or informally.

This means that you may only hear of interesting new posts or opportunities through the 'office grapevine', and that means talking to people. However, you can't necessarily expect to learn all you need to know in one conversation, or even from just one person. You will probably need to build up your contacts and increase your visibility for quite a while before you see any real results.

This doesn't always mean talking about work – in fact, someone may remember you because of a shared hobby, or because you talked so enthusiastically and knowledgeably about a recent event. In a work environment, you are more likely to talk about work, but it doesn't rule out a conversation about other interests.

Building up professional contacts doesn't just mean talking to the colleagues you work with on a daily basis. It may mean moving into other departments, asking questions, talking to those senior to you and telling them, when appropriate, what you're looking for and what your ambitions are.

Networking in the workplace, if done in the right way, is not only acceptable but vital. In fact, you are likely to gain respect from others as they become more aware of you on a professional level.

> *I am steadily building a professional diary and attending different training days and short courses. I use these days for networking and I have also started to research self-employment, contacting my tax office for further information.*
>
> Jan, UK

" *Having spent sixteen satisfying, challenging and enjoyable years as a full-time member of BBC Northern Ireland, I faced my last day with my colleagues and couldn't help asking myself, 'What have I done?' It was my decision to leave, to start my own training consultancy business, but I knew it would mean building up a whole new network of professional contacts for myself. That was a great challenge for me.* **"**

Gloria Gilfillan, Springboard Trainer, Northern Ireland

Mentors

Some companies have a formal mentoring system offering their employees the chance to have a mentor. A mentor is usually someone senior in the company who is willing to meet with a more junior person and offer advice, support, contacts and other career help.

If there is no such opportunity where you work, or if you are not employed in a company, you may like to consider setting up a mentoring arrangement for yourself. You would need to make a list of all the people who might be suitable mentors for you, or those people who might know a suitable mentor for you.

66 *One day the university training officer, who had become a kind of personal mentor and continued to show an interest in my work ...approached me and asked whether I would be willing to consider becoming a licensed trainer for the Springboard programme... What a gift!* **99**

Pam Day, Springboard Trainer, UK

NOTEBOOK

A MENTOR FOR YOU

Jot down the names of some people who you think would be a good mentor for you. Having this list will help you to focus on the areas where you need advice and support.

Add to the list as you meet new people.

At a later stage, you may wish to ask one of them to mentor you, or they may simply be a role model.

As with friends, choose your mentor carefully. Be clear about what you want from the mentoring relationship and how you see it working. Take advice from others who have experience in this area, or get more information – the book 'Networking & Mentoring for Women' by Lily Segerman-Peck is a great place to start.

> *My boss is a woman and my mentor at the moment. She is great at giving me feedback and encouraging me as well as challenging me and my doubts. She is my inspiration for good leadership and has encouraged me to become more visible in my organisation. This gives me excellent contacts.*
>
> Camilla, Denmark

Coaching

Nowadays, coaching doesn't happen only in sport – it's a very effective resource for self-development. There are professional coaches but there are also less formal arrangements, such as coaching partnerships between work colleagues or friends.

The ideal coach is positive, encouraging and always on your side. You might decide to find a coach because you want support for a specific goal or project, or you might want to 'bounce ideas' off someone who will listen and respond objectively.

Your coach is in equal partnership with you in your coaching relationship. This might be in person, by telephone or by email, and some people prefer the anonymity of a coach they never actually meet. Being coached by someone you know can be a good alternative if you find the right person and agree some groundrules from the start.
A good coach is almost like an extension of yourself – a voice that will remind you of what you said you want to achieve, and will give the encouragement to get there.

You may find that there is a coaching system where you work, or you may decide to try a coaching partnership with someone you know. If, however, you want to find an independent coach, the best place to look is on the Internet, where there are plenty of resources for coaching.

Networks, formal and informal

Firstly, formal networks. No matter where you live, there is a huge variety of formal networks that you can join, and these might be local, national or international. Formal groups are likely to have regular meetings or events, someone responsible for finances or membership, and a joining process, and they are likely to have a specific aim in mind.

For example, if your goal is to further your career in marketing, it is worth finding out about The Marketing Guild and similar groups that put you in contact with other professionals already working in that field. If your goal is to widen your circle of friends, it may be worth joining a group that you share an interest with – such as a businesswomen's network or writers' circle.

Networks do not need to be about work. Networks range from Women's Institute branches and Mother-and-Toddler groups to specialist interests, such as wine-tasting or local history.

I was working in a very difficult climate of disapproval, so I looked beyond work to realise my personal self-worth. I was invited to join the local Scouting Movement as a Cub Leader, and enjoyed three years working with other adults who were accepting and supportive.

Cate, Australia

There are also activity-based networks, such as book-clubs, snowboarding, creative-writing circles, Choral Societies or environmental campaign groups.

Whatever your interest, favourite activity or passion, you can probably find someone else keen to share the experience.

Informally, you probably network already, simply by connecting with people that you know, or offering help to others through your own resources. Women are particularly skilful at networking – but often less skilled at recognising that this is what they are doing!

Members of a network usually offer their help and support to each other in some way.

Networks are a way of sharing information, whether it is at the school gate, the office canteen or in professional groups.

Interacting with women from other organisations provided me with an insight into the role of networking and how it can strengthen my commitment to achieving career aspirations.

Ms Nisha Jain, India

Networking is a means of getting myself and my needs out in circulation and hopefully raising my profile with the people who make the decisions.

Linda, UK

Why networks are so important

We are now more likely to leave the place where we grew up, and to move frequently during a lifetime.

This means that we cannot always rely on the community or family to be our primary support, so we need to build up new networks.

I have learned that other people are reluctant to network and have not used their contacts and friends when necessary. Many are surprised when they happen to mention their predicament and find that other people know of someone who may be able to help them. There are others out there in a similar position who are willing to help.

Lynne, UK

NOTEBOOK

YOUR NETWORKS

Draw a diagram of your current networks – a small circle in the middle of the page to represent you, then draw spokes outwards, like a bicycle wheel.

Each spoke stands for one network that you belong to. You may have spokes for some or all of the networks mentioned earlier.

Look at your diagram critically and ask yourself if your networks are providing you with the support and resources you need.

Valerie Everitt

I read about the Springboard Programme in 'Good Housekeeping' and 'Women and Training News' in 1991. This, I discovered only recently, was one of the first public Springboard programmes, and it was a very special time for me. I realised that only I could ever make things happen but I could and should ask for the help and support I needed to make life better for me and everyone around me.

My personal key to change was networking. Meeting women from outside my own narrow professional circle had been of great value and fun. I set myself the target of identifying a network in Cambridge where I lived and, if one didn't exist, forming one myself. Several phone calls later I had had no success, then a chance read of the local newspaper brought me exactly what I was looking for. An invitation to an evening to re-launch an East Anglian Businesswomen's Network in the city.

The rest followed on easily. I joined the group, volunteered for the committee, got involved in organising training events and made some excellent friends who shared my interests in women's development.

Springboard made me realise that we all view ourselves in a distorted way, and lack confidence in our abilities, the very abilities that the other group members could see plainly, and admired.

Anne, UK

Valerie Everitt's story is a wonderful example of combining personal contacts with wider resources. Valerie found out about Springboard through articles in a magazine and a professional publication and she then achieved her goals through setting targets, noticing a relevant article in a newspaper and building on networks.

A network checklist

Ask yourself:-

- Do you have a mix of old and new contacts?

- Are you meeting people who are totally different from you – different departments or with different backgrounds?

- What do you do to keep your contacts up-to-date?

- Do you belong to any formal or professional networks?

- Do you check that your networking time is spent with energy-givers and good role models, not 'moaning Minnies'?

I had joined the Home Economics Association and undertaken various speaking engagements and cookery demonstrations for them. Through this connection, a friend of a friend suggested that I should apply for a position with the Technical and Further Education College, as they wanted someone to teach health and nutrition – which I did. Always build your networks and look out for new opportunities in unexpected places.

Chris, Australia

Tips for good networking

- Be certain about your own standards and values. You need to have a clear idea of who you are and what is important to you if you want to interact successfully with others.

- Recognise - and <u>appreciate</u> - your own achievements and skills. These are what you can offer to others.

- Keep a written list of your goals, both short and long term, to remind yourself of what you need. This will help you to be aware of what you're looking for from your networks and who might be able to help you.

- Be aware of your image and behaviour. This may mean changing the ways in which you present yourself in different settings. Some networks will work better for you if you adopt a low-key, friendly approach, while others may call for more formal, professional conduct.

- Have an effective way of introducing yourself. Again, this may vary in different situations. When people ask, "What do you do?", you need to have an answer that is brief but assertive. *Never* along the lines of "Oh, I'm just a secretary..." but rather "I manage......" and put into businesslike words whatever it is you do. Everybody manages their job – it's just what they manage that varies. In other words, talk yourself up, not down.

- If being in a group of strangers makes you nervous, build your confidence by being well prepared. Have some opening remarks or questions ready – if need be, practise beforehand. Remember that others are nervous too (even if they don't look it!) and concentrate on making them feel comfortable with you.

- Take the initiative. If you go into a room where everyone seems to be deep in conversation, check first if there is anyone standing alone to whom you could introduce yourself. If not, choose a group rather than a couple, and hover on the edge. It is likely that you will be noticed and drawn into the conversation. If this doesn't happen, drift away and try another group. Listen to what the conversation is about and venture a remark when there's a pause.

- Look on all these situations as a game you're playing and see how good you can get at it. Remember, it's you who are in control and you who decides who you would like to network with. Keep in mind: 'The important thing is not what they think of me, but what I think of them'. As with many things, it gets a little easier every time you try it.

People Power

You may feel that you can't ask other people for help, but think about how you react when someone asks your advice on something – you probably feel flattered to be asked. It is true that most of the people you know will be happy to help if you ask them, and only very few would not want to.

> *We all need help – you just can't do it all on your own!*
>
> Terri, Australia

Of course, even when you do think that you could benefit from the help, advice or experience of the people you know, they are not likely to realise their ability to help you unless you ask.

" *I've made a big discovery. When I was setting up a Springboard programme, I wrote the leaflets and brochures, I phoned and talked to the company and organised everything, always thinking 'Why don't they do anything?'*

Now I know the secret: it's because I always thought they would find out themselves what help I would need. Of course they didn't. Now I say what I need. And they do it. That makes life much easier. **"**

Karin Blauensteiner, Springboard Trainer, Austria

Be aware of the people around you, what they have to offer, how they can help you – and don't be modest about what you have to offer others.

Never take your gifts for granted, and never guard them too closely.

Imagine if everybody could share their skills and gifts with others – it would be as if we all had these abilities and qualities ourselves.

> *I have found that others are interested in what I have to say and they even seek me out to ask me my opinion and also for help. People are willing to help you, but you have to ask, as they aren't mind readers!*
>
> Claire, UK

" *Every person you meet, every soul you come into contact with, you can learn from. But also, you are a special individual yourself – and you have something unique to offer to every person you meet. It is good to be open to this - it is how we all grow and develop.* **"**

Sonja, Austrian Guest Speaker for Springboard

Chapter Five
Net Gains

'Women world-wide are now exploring the potential of the Internet.'

Women Connect

Surfing the Net   **Sending an email**   **Shopping online**

Not many years ago, these phrases would have meant very little to most people. Now they are everyday expressions to some, and strike fear into the hearts of others.

If you are one of those who has the Internet at her fingertips, some of this chapter may seem basic, but don't skip it. You are a pioneer to whom many may look for guidance. You may find here what you need to help others become part of the Net-wise 21st century.

To those of you whose reaction was a sinking heart and a groan, don't despair. What you read here may make a big difference to your life - hopefully for the better.

What's all the fuss about?

Imagine a huge room, so vast you cannot see where it begins or ends, and you cannot see the ceiling.

Imagine that this room is full of books, research reports, newspapers, company information, and even shops – everything you can imagine, representing every country in the world.

Imagine that you could walk in and find out anything you want to know. You just sit down, choose a word to say what you're looking for, and someone brings you all the references. Then you click a button and look at exactly what you want.

That is one way of seeing the Internet – an Aladdin's Cave that you can walk into. No matter who you are or where you live, you can access all of this and you can even contribute to it for other people to see. That's what all the fuss is about.

The Internet – what have you heard?

"The Net's impossible to understand."
Not these days – there are hundreds of magazines, courses and books dedicated to telling you how to get started on the Internet, and use it effectively.

"It's addictive."
It can be addictive because there is so much to explore, but it doesn't have to be – alcohol can be addictive yet plenty of people enjoy it in moderation.

"It's full of disgusting porn."
Yes, there is some unpleasant stuff on the Internet, because anyone can 'publish' onto it, and there are (as yet) few restrictions. However, there are ways of blocking out certain material, and protecting children against it.

"I haven't got a computer and I can't afford one."
You don't have to buy anything – try your nearest college, library or cybercafé. You may pay a small fee per hour, or it may be free. Computers and Internet connections are becoming more and more affordable, and you will very soon be able to access the Internet through your TV or even a mobile phone.

> *The best attitude is that technology is a game; have fun with it, don't get frustrated, play with it.*
>
> Donna, USA

"It's only for spotty youths or nerds."
Absolutely not. It's becoming an essential tool for business, for research, for shopping, and even for finding a new job.

"It's a waste of time and bad for your eyes."
Like any interest, it's only a time-waster if you allow it to be. If used well, it can <u>save</u> you time, money and effort. And it's only bad for your eyes if you don't give yourself plenty of breaks from the screen.

The Good, the Bad and the Ugly

With anything as powerful and all-encompassing as the Internet, there are problems as well as benefits:

- Anyone can use it, so anyone can misuse or abuse it.
- No-one controls it, so there are no universal rules.
- It is empowering, so it can give power to the wrong people.
- Anyone can communicate, so what is communicated is unlimited.
- There is a free exchange of ideas, which is very difficult to censor.
- It is trans-national – there are no geographical boundaries.
- It has a levelling effect – everyone is equal.
- Net-surfing can result in nasty shocks or some wonderful surprises.

Caught up in the Net

We intend to show you at least some of what you're missing if you don't yet access the Internet – or 'Net'.

To make use of the Net, you don't need to know how it started or how it works. The important things are what you can do with it and why you need to become familiar with it.

It is estimated that by the year 2005, 2 billion people will be using the Net and they will encompass 90% of the world's buying power.

Net-haves and Net-have-nots

There is a huge danger of the world becoming divided into 'Net-haves' and 'Net-have-nots'. The Net is another source of power and influence, so women particularly must ensure that they are part of these technological advances.

Using the Net will become cheaper and more accessible very quickly. Knowing how to use it will also be a career essential for most jobs in the near future.

Information technology in general is changing the face of work as we know it, but particularly so with the Internet. Even job-hunting and job advertising happen increasingly on the Net.

People who insist that they are 'technophobes' will be consigning themselves to unemployability. So if you don't have the skills, get them – preferably by requesting training at work or signing up to a local college course.

What the Net offers:

- **A worldwide community** – The Global Village is becoming a reality. You can join any community you want to, from wherever you are. Without moving physically, you can join a new home town or a new community via the Net.

- **Free exchange of information** – You can take what you need from the sum total of information and you can also add to it.

> *I was terrified of the Internet until I had one try. It was much easier than I'd imagined! Train times, holidays, even buying a car – now I use it whenever I can.*
>
> Rachel, UK

- **Business opportunities** – The Net provides, at minimal cost, a platform for anyone to market themselves or their business. It's a level playing field for all businesses whatever their size or scope. The big corporations have the same presence on the Net as a small, one-woman business – it all comes under the banner of 'e-commerce' (electronic commerce). There are great opportunities to find a niche and make money, and there's no reason why a good website can't make good business.

- **Shopping** – This may be what you have heard most about. You can search the Internet for almost anything you want to buy – even through to your supermarket essentials. And with the Internet you can buy instantly from almost anywhere in the world.

- **Pressure groups** – A chance to join others who want to make a difference and bring about changes in the world. Action groups can be formed, organised and make their presence felt via the Net – a huge audience of billions waiting to be contacted. Proof of their power is the fact that certain governments ban or jam sites because they fear their influence.

- **Electronic democracy** – Soon, technology will allow an instant electronic response and people will be able to register their votes on a wide range of issues, via an electronic keypad. This may mean the end of politics as we know it – and an end to women's struggle to be fully represented in parliament?

Start with Email

Electronic mail is most people's introduction to the wonderful world of the web. There are many ways in which you can get your own email address, allowing you to send and read email from any Net-linked computer in the world.

Sending and receiving email has many advantages over 'snail mail' (post) or the conventional telephone – it's delivered instantaneously and allows the recipient to pick up and respond to messages at her own convenience. Of course email doesn't replace more conventional methods of communication, but it's a fantastic new addition to the 'people-talking-to-people' processes.

What's your interest?

Here are some suggested websites to visit – only a minuscule selection of the vast riches available, and they are changing every day. We've deliberately not given you any further information – no point in telling the treasure hunters beforehand what they're going to find!

At home?	www.fmb.org.uk	www.improveline.com
	www.upmystreet.com	www.diy.co.uk
	www.foodndrink.co.uk	www.interiorinternet.co.uk
In the garden?	www.oxalis.co.uk	www.rhs.org.uk

Keen on books? www.amazon.co.uk www.bol.co.uk
www.whsmith.co.uk www.bibliofind.com
www.promo.net/pg/pgframed_index.html

Buying a car? www.autobytel.co.uk www.carseller.co.uk
www.carbusters.com www.oneswoop.com

Planning a journey? www.rac.co.uk www.theaa.co.uk
www.multimap.com www.thetrainline.com
www.cheapflights.co.uk www.bargainflight.co.uk

Need a holiday? www.lastminute.com www.bargainholidays.com
www.deckchair.com www.travelstore.com
www.a2btravel.com www.holiday.co.uk
www.laterooms.com www.holidaybank.co.uk

Going travelling? www.fco.gov.uk www.tips4trips.com
www.totaltravel.net www.eurotrip.com

Want a night out? www.ticketmaster.co.uk www.uk-calling.co.uk
www.uktw.co.uk www.aloud.com
www.goodpubs.co.uk www.countyweb.co.uk

Need some culture? www.moma.org www.24hourmuseum.org.uk
www.artguide.org www.museumsworld.com

Going shopping? www.buy.co.uk www.letsbuyit.com
www.shopspy.co.uk www.shopsmart.com

Looking for a job? www.totaljobs.com www.gradunet.co.uk
www.jobtrack.co.uk www.jobsite.co.uk
www.jobsearch.co.uk www.overseasjobs.com
www.jobsunlimited.co.uk www.monster.co.uk

Got children?	www.learnfree.co.uk	www.eduweb.co.uk
	www.revisions.co.uk	www.familyeducation.com
	www.yahooligans.com	www.kidscom.com
	www.howstuffworks.com	www.crayola.com

| **Fancy a bargain?** | www.qxl.com | www.firedup.com |
| | www.fsauctions.com | www.aucland.co.uk |

| **Maturing nicely?** | www.silverhairs.co.uk | www.vavo.co.uk |
| | www.idf50.com | www.u3a.org.uk |

| **Managing money?** | www.pankhurst.co.uk | www.fionaprice.co.uk |

Women's issues?	www.f-mail.demon.co.uk	www.wwwomen.com
	www.women.com	www.womenfolk.com
	www.handbag.com	www.cybergrrl.com
	www.beme.com	www.charlottestreet.com
	www.wnas.org.uk	www.reddirect.co.uk

And of course,

www.springingforward.com

Having such a huge number of sites and such a vast amount of information at the mere click of a mouse can be overwhelming. If you're a beginner, it may be a good idea to find and 'bookmark' (or 'Favourite') about a dozen sites that provide you with what you need, are easy to navigate around and are regularly updated.

You can find virtually anything on the Net if you use good search engines. The best include www.ukplus.com, www.yahoo.co.uk, www.ask.co.uk and www.google.com.

What are women doing with the Net?

Almost as many women as men are now using the Net. Women currently account for about 40% of the online population, and this looks set to increase rapidly in the next few years.

Women are said to be more task-orientated than men when using the Internet. Rather than just browsing for leisure, we are more likely to use it as a time-saver for getting information or solving problems.

" *It is often said that women network only in a social sense with close friends and family and so miss out on ideas, influence and information from the wider world. The Net is an easier way for women to be 'in the know' without physically having to go somewhere else, in lives that are often jam-packed already.* **"**

Christine Baines, Springboard Trainer, UK

For proactive involvement in women's concerns, there are sites like Virtual Sisterhood (www.igc.org/vsister). This site is committed to breaking down the barriers that exist on the web for women world-wide. It aims to encourage women to use the Net not just as consumers of information but as activists.

Women are beginning to discover and make the most of this new access to knowledge, to power and to communities around the globe. If there is something you particularly want to see on the Internet, you can always publish it yourself....

Go and get netted!

In this chapter, you may have noticed that there are no 'Notebook' sections. Instead, it's an encouragement to use technology rather than the traditional pen and paper.

This book could not easily have been written without the use of emails and the research made possible by the Internet. It meant that no matter where we were geographically, or what time of day we preferred to work, we could send work directly to each other, and could receive stories or information instantly from women across the world.

The Internet is a phenomenal resource.

It is open to everyone and is not discriminatory – you can access the same information as other people, regardless of your age, race, sex, physical abilities, even what you're wearing!

If you haven't really explored the Internet yet, set yourself a time when you will at least give it a go. Only then can you really know how you feel about it – and maybe you, too, will be singing its praises to other people.

" *Created by men, the Net often remains the province of men. But just as there came a time to take control of the TV remote, it's now time for women to get netted - and the only way to do this is to go on, get out there and get started. If you feel embarrassed about 'not being in the know', put on some dark glasses, pull on a big hat and call in at an internet café.*

There'll be someone there just delighted to help you get on line. And within a very short space of time, you'll be logging on with the rest of us. **"**

Mary Gray, Diversity UK

Chapter Six
Gathering Momentum

'Making the leap from burning desire to reality means working out what it will take to fulfil your dream and allowing yourself to go out and do it.'

Zoe, Australia

This chapter looks at some practical steps to maximise your chances of success – and to keep them high.

Use it for a starting burst of energy, an extra boost, support, or simply ideas to come back to.

The areas that we'll cover are:

1. Getting organised
2. Making decisions
3. Setting limits
4. Facing fear
5. Dealing with money issues
6. Simplifying your life
7. Looking after yourself
8. Communicating with others
9. Finding and using your strength
10. Enjoying it all!

All these are immense subjects in their own right. Some of them may not be a problem for you. There are plenty of resources to help you in a more detailed way with the particular issues that are challenging for you, but here are some pointers.

1. Getting organised

People vary between those who love being thoroughly organised and hate any type of mess and those who love mess and find it extremely difficult to be thoroughly organised!

Listen to (audio tape):
Getting Organized — Stephanie Winston

Visit:
www.juliemorgenstern.com

Even if you are not at either of those two extremes, you will find yourself tending to one side or the other. It's almost impossible – and probably not very wise – to attempt to change yourself completely. The best plan is to work with whatever style comes naturally to you. If you find yourself letting the mess pile up until you need a real blitz to sort everything, go with this method. If you hate even a hair being out of place, set aside time regularly to keep things as tidy as you wish.

Why organise?

The main purpose of being organised is to spend time doing the things that really matter rather than waste it looking for missing items or sorting through the muddle. Here are a few tips:

- Don't attempt to fit yourself into other people's methods of doing things – find a system that suits **you**.

- Clear out the clutter – until you are happy with the way your system is working, set aside a regular time every day simply to CHUCK STUFF OUT. If you can't bear to because you fear you'll lose something precious, remind yourself of what you really value and ask yourself 'Is this something I could never replace if I really needed it?' For example, whatever is in your newspaper cuttings file could probably be found on the Net.

- If you have a computer at home, use it. There's software that will keep all your contacts sorted, remind you of dates, act as a diary, and lots more. Again, set aside time to find out what your PC can do or get a PC-expert friend to show you – it'll save time in the long run.

- Make organising fun – use colourful folders, colour-coded reference systems, a cheerful jingle on your computer to remind you of times and dates.

- Don't allow others to sabotage your system – get them on board, show them how your system works and insist that they conform. Expect to do the same for them.

Remember – when you've had a major (or minor) achievement in 'getting organised', treat yourself to a reward... as long as it doesn't involve more clutter!

2. Making decisions

Few people are taught how to make decisions and we are actively discouraged from making decisions without oodles of advice from so-called 'experts'.

> **Read:**
> *"Yes" or "No": The Guide to Better Decisions* – Spencer Johnson
>
> *Making Decisions* – Dean Juniper
>
> **Visit:** www.decidenow.com

Of course we all need enough information to help us with certain decisions, but too often even these experts cannot agree. The result is that we are often the victims of 'paralysis by analysis' and simply give up. We end up not feeling able to trust our own judgement in even minor matters. Here's a simple formula – **3Rs** - for helping your decision-making process:

1. **Result** - Ask yourself, "What result do I want to see?" Visualise it as clearly as you can and write down what you want to be the end product.

2. **Retrace** - Work backward from this end product asking yourself, "What needs to happen for this result to occur?" Plan the steps back to the present and write down the first step that needs to be taken.

3. **Resolve** - Decide to take that step. As with so much of life, if it's broken down into small steps, it's easier to start on.

> *One day, I came out of the salon where I worked in Austria, I looked to the sky, and I felt, "Yes, I must go to Switzerland". I decided that I would move there. Within two weeks, I had met someone who knew of a job perfect for me, based in Switzerland, and that was that.*
>
> Sonja, Austrian Guest speaker for Springboard

> *The pivotal point for me was when I actually took control of my career and decided what I wanted and how I was going to get it.*
>
> Karen, UK

> **"** *In the last six months, I have made some big and important decisions. I am sure that these decisions have been growing little by little inside me, so that I might find the solutions to my problems when the time was right.* **"**
>
> Pirkko, Springboard Trainer, Finland

3. Setting limits

Are you a jelly fish or a jam jar? Are you swayed by any passing tide, pushed around without any firm rules about what you will allow and what you won't? Or do you have a clear profile, able to define who you are and what you stand for?

Setting limits is about making it clear what people may do or say to you, and what they may not. It also means being clear about the terms on which you permit people to enter your life.

Read:
The Assertiveness Workbook
– Joanna Gutmann

Listen to:
Boundaries: When to Say Yes/When to Say No...
– Henry Cloud and John Townsend

Visit: www.topten.org

You are probably familiar with the concept of 'personal space' and how uncomfortable it is when someone invades it, uninvited. As you become more aware of who you want to be, an essential skill is to set limits not just on your physical space but on your mental and emotional space as well.

NOTEBOOK

KNOW YOUR LIMITS

Decide what behaviour in other people is acceptable to you and what isn't.

Make your decisions based on your highest standards.

Decide exactly what you will say or do if someone oversteps your limits.

This is a matter of assertive behaviour – communicating clearly to others, while demonstrating an understanding of their needs too.

Write down what you would do or say, and make a commitment to that.

With clear limits, you gain a more healthy life for yourself. They help you to grow by reducing the wastage of time and energy on others. Some people will like you less, others will become far more attracted to you and respect you a lot more.

Don't expect the setting of your new limits to be an enjoyable experience either for you or for others involved. People who have been used to treating you exactly as they wish will find it difficult to change and will blame you, probably for being 'selfish'. But you will find it is worth it in the long run.

I've decided that I quite like myself as a person and that, given that I like myself, I deserve to be treated well, both by myself and others. This is not something that had previously filtered through into my consciousness!

Anne, UK

4. Facing fear

What are our greatest fears?

- Fear that we won't be loved, won't be secure, can't cope on our own.
- Fear that we don't deserve success.
- Fear of not having enough – money, work or love.
- Fear of failing.
- Fear of what people will think of us.
- Fear that we aren't good enough.

> **Read:**
> *Feel the Fear and Do It Anyway* – Susan Jeffers
>
> **Listen to:**
> *The Art of Fearbusting* – Susan Jeffers
>
> **Visit:**
> www.emotiontoolkit.com

Even very successful women admit to feeling a fraud, an imposter, not fit to be in the position they've attained.

Reality is our own creation, and so are our fears. Fear is highly repetitive and addictive. Fear has one positive side – it stops us hurting ourselves – but if it's unchecked, it can stop us doing anything. How many people have decided 'not to, just in case..'?

Overcoming fear involves complete trust in ourselves, not that we won't ever make mistakes but that we can handle whatever comes along. Being afraid of things doesn't stop them happening – in fact, we attract what we dwell on. This is why top athletes are trained to put any thoughts of failure out of their minds, and to focus only on winning. We make what we think.

Forget fear – think excitement!

If fear is so dreadful, why do some people go out of their way to create it deliberately? Why the huge popularity of horror films, dangerous sports and theme park rollercoasters? Because fear equals excitement – you can become excited about the thing you are afraid of. When you're afraid, ask yourself, "How can I change my view of this fear and turn it into excitement?"

Ways to give your courage a boost:

- Regularly sharing your dreams with positive friends helps.

- Seek out courage-building opportunities.

- Take control of your response to fear. Never deny fear – allow yourself to feel it, then remind your feelings of the new response –acknowledge it, recognise it, even welcome it, but still take the action you fear.

- Imagine and plan for the 'worst case scenario' – find a way to deal with that, and anything else is a breeze!

- Use your chosen techniques to calm the physical symptoms of fear.

- Use creative visualisation: see your dream for real.

- Give yourself plenty of practice in facing and overcoming fears – regular, practical stretching.

" *I was on walking holiday in the French Alps. The setting was a misty afternoon in the Mount Viso region. The only way down the mountain was to cross a very steep glacier holding onto a rope while manoeuvring my feet along a narrow six-inch icy path and at the same time balancing a rucksack weighing 30lbs. I experienced the real meaning of 'Feel the fear and do it anyway' and reached the other side!* **"**

Gloria Gilfillan,
Springboard Trainer,
Northern Ireland

I sometimes lack confidence and have a fear of failure. I know it often feels easier to stay in a comfortable rut, and I have a history of putting things off and of passivity. Being aware of my patterns of behaviour and continuing to push and encourage myself keeps me moving forward.

Jan, UK

" *I am always scared before an important presentation. I prepare as well as possible, I pray intensively beforehand and I arrive early. I take a CD player along and I put on the music I like while I prepare the room and the people are arriving. Then the presentation goes well.* **"**

Karen Blauensteiner, Springboard Trainer, Austria

5. Dealing with money issues

The best way to deal with money issues is to become financially independent as quickly as possible.

This doesn't mean slogging away at a job you hate just to save enough to feel secure, although you may decide to do this for a certain length of time. It may be the right thing for you as long as you keep your eye on your light at the end of the tunnel. It does mean consistently saving a proportion of your income, no less than 10%, regularly, consistently and into a place where you can't touch it without great difficulty.

It also means taking time and trouble to learn about investments, mortgages and pensions, all subjects that women traditionally have not had to think seriously about. It's just one reason why many women still have big problems around the issue of money.

Read:
Swimming With Piranha Makes You Hungry
– Colin Turner

16 Steps to Financial Success –
W. Patrick Naylor

Managing Your Personal Finances - John Claxton

Listen to:
Creating Affluence –
Deepak Chopra

Visit:
www.fool.co.uk

www.armchairmillionaire.com

Money, money, money...

- If you're in a position where you find it impossible to save anything, at least make yourself stay within your budget. Give yourself an allowance and stick to it.

- Money in itself is neutral, like power. It is a type of energy that can be used for good or evil. If you opened yourself up to more of this energy, how would you use it?

- Like confidence, you have to assume you've got it before you get it. Act as if you know the money will be there for the important things you need to do. Take the first steps and the money will follow.

NOTEBOOK

KNOW YOUR MONEY HANG-UPS

Write a heading of 'What I Think and Feel About Money'. List everything that comes into your head without stopping to think.

Later on, consider what you've written and assess your answers.

Is your attitude to money positive or negative? Do you have an 'Abundance Mentality' – that's there plenty of it to go around and some of it will definitely be coming your way?

Do you feel that you will never have enough? You will – if you are determined to.

- Having lots of money never made anybody safe from tragedy or secure for the whole of life. Tragedies can happen to anyone and money can come and go. Your only real security is in being confident in yourself to survive anything that life can throw at you. And if you believe you can, you can!

- The best investment you can make is in yourself. Find new ways to expand your knowledge, widen your experience, learn new skills. None of this need cost a lot of money and it will yield dividends in the future.

66
I took a part-time job in administration to give me some free time to develop my training work; this was a big step for me as I was reluctant to give up the security and independence of a full-time salary. However, I knew it was the only way to move forward.... **99**

Pam Day, Springboard Trainer, UK

At the time, the courses in which I was interested were cost-prohibitive... This initial setback did not deter me and in September 1994 I began a ten week Introductory Certificate in Supervisory Management at North Tyneside College. For me that was the start of my journey of self-discovery.

Karen, UK

---

6. Simplifying your life

Why is simplifying a good way to make changes in your life? It's not a new idea but it's becoming more attractive as life in the 21st century looks like being even more frenetic and demanding than in the 20th Century.

Simplifying doesn't mean you have to move to the wilds of the countryside, grow your own vegetables, get some oil lamps and have a loo at the bottom of the garden. It may mean this to a few people but for most of us, it means taking a long hard look at our lifestyle and working out where we can 'downshift'.

Read:
Getting a Life – Polly Ghazi and Judy Jones

Listen to:
The Elaine St James Value Collection: Simplify Your Life, Living the Simple Life, Inner Simplicity – Elaine St James

NOTEBOOK

YOUR LIFESTYLE

Work out how much of your income goes on keeping you in your job.
What do you spend on travel, clothes, keeping fit and looking good, childcare, and all the other items which you must have to keep up the 'professional' image and service your way of living?
How many times do you 'treat' yourself because your job has over-burdened you?

Where could you make changes?
It's easier to start, as usual, with small steps.

Keep it simple

We've already looked at 'de-cluttering' – it's a very good place to start, but it's still only a beginning. Other ways in which you might consider simplifying your life are:

- Keep asking yourself the question, 'If I do this/buy this/join this/agree to this, will it simplify my life?' If the answer is no, don't be tempted and maintain your limits!

- Consider your job from all angles. Is it really what you want to do? Could you go part-time and do more of what you love? Could you save travel costs? Might you consider asking to work from home or even going freelance?

- Use the technology you have to make life easier, not more stressful. If you have a mobile phone, make sure you're the one who decides when it should be switched on. You don't have to be at the beck and call of everyone all the time. Use your computer to keep all the information you need easily available – but also make sure it's backed up regularly.

You may find it's difficult at first to adjust to a more simple way of life, but stick with it. Most changes are hard to assimilate at first, so do it at a rate that suits you.

Some people find that to make one or two big changes – for example, selling the car and using a bike, or moving to a smaller house – gives them a huge boost and an impetus to keep going along the road to less and less materially. What life then gives you is more and more spiritually.

7. Looking after yourself

Your body is your life. Nothing happens to you without your body being involved. This sounds so obvious, but so much of what we do and how we think excludes any consideration of the body. At last we are seeing progress in the medical profession about the importance of the whole person and how each area of our life can impact on another because the body is the common factor. So how do you treat your body?

> **Read:**
> *Achieving Personal Well-Being* – James Chalmers
>
> **Listen to:**
> *Love Your Body* – Louise L. Hay
>
> **Visit:**
> www.get-motivated.com
>
> www.healthnet.org.uk

When you treat your body well, you have better access to the rest of you – your heart, mind and soul. This is not the place to lecture you on what you probably know already. But don't force yourself to diet or give up smoking or stop eating chocolate, or any one of a host of 'shoulds' we batter ourselves with. Instead, learn to love your body – easier said than done, but not impossible when the other changes you're making come together.

Some ways of treating your body well:

- Have your hair done professionally – and often.

- Have the occasional manicure, massage or beauty treatment. If you can't afford a professional, team up with a friend and do it for each other. There are plenty of books and videos around to help.

- Try different ways of exercising your body until you find one or more that really suits you. If you hate the hassle of getting undressed, don't bother with swimming. If you love the open air, take regular walks or bike rides. If you need more motivation than your own, find a friend who wants the company too and keep each other on track.

Looking after yourself also involves having time to yourself, doing things you enjoy just because you want to, and protecting yourself from damaging influences. This may include people – so set limits. It may also include reducing commitments that drain your energy, and redesigning your way of life to fit the person you really want to be.

> *I would like to play golf and I'm looking forward to having outdoor me-time. I know it will be difficult to find the time on a regular basis but I am entitled to have time to myself and I will arrange a time each week and tell my family about it.*
>
> Lynne, UK

8. Communicating with others

Deciding to make changes is one thing – telling others about it is often more difficult, particularly to your nearest and dearest.

An intimate relationship often reacts against change, possibly because if you change, they may fear you want them to change as well.

Read:
You Just Don't Understand – Deborah Tannen

Listen to:
Conversation Power – James F. Van Fleet

If you are serious about becoming more of who you want to be, it's important to find your voice and the right words to express yourself. The qualities you need to communicate well with others include:

- listening without interrupting
- saying what you want without bullying or complaining
- expressing your feelings without letting the feelings take over
- being considerate of the other person's needs and opinions without belittling them

Sounds like a tall order? The answer is simply to be more aware of how you communicate and take small steps to doing it better.

Even for people who have worked on communication skills, this is crucial: no-one communicates so perfectly that she is never misunderstood, never offends anyone and never says 'That isn't what I meant at all!'

> *I found it difficult to speak up and give my views about something, the main reason being that I didn't think anybody would want to listen to what I had to say.*
>
> Claire, UK

Crystal Clear

- When you're listening to someone, really concentrate on them, put yourself in their shoes and see how the world looks from their standpoint. Ask questions to clarify what they're saying but also to show you're giving them your full attention.

- If you really want a big challenge, try to listen for one whole day without judging or criticising anyone. This doesn't mean you have to agree with them, but you do have to have what Edward de Bono calls the "Yes, and...." response rather than "Yes, but...." In other words, agree with them and add your opinion to theirs. Not always easy!

- Keep focussed on the main issue you want to discuss. Don't be led astray into other byways and don't be tempted to use the "....and *another* thing..." tactic.

- Be prepared for criticism – not everyone will be having a non-judgemental day! Criticism always hurts, when it's not deserved and even more so when it is. Practise being aware of your feelings, accepting them and moving on. If you don't feel ready to talk about the criticism straightaway, ask for more time and to discuss it later.

- Select role models to study – people whose communication skills you admire. Look, listen and learn from what they do, what they say and how they use body language effectively.

I have discussed my intentions with my family and I know I will have to depend on them to help me with the household tasks. I will have to trust them and give them the responsibility, so that I have more time to study and revise.

Linda, UK

9. Finding and using your true strength

Think of your true strength as being your capacity to achieve something, your ability to contribute something and your energy to get stuck in and make something happen. That's what we mean here by *strength*.

To make the changes you've decided on you'll need strength. Feeling strong isn't a constant state for any of us. It fluctuates from day to day, even from hour to hour. We can accept this but also do something to help the strength flow when we really need it. Some of the feelings that sap our strength include guilt, fear, isolation and stress.

Read:
Woman Power
– Lynda Field

The Confidence to be Yourself – Brian Roet

Listen to:
Personal Power –
Lisa Ford

Increase Your Confidence - Gael Lindenfield

NOTEBOOK

FEEL THE POWER

In your notebook, write down some of the occasions when you have felt powerless.
What were the reasons for this lack of strength?

Now note down times when you felt strong and capable.
What were the reasons for your strength at these times?

Choose one of the occasions when you felt strong and allow yourself to remember it completely – relive it for a while.
How does it feel? Recognise and enjoy the sensation of being strong – draw from this when you are in need of a boost.

Awareness of when and why we feel unable to act helps us to recognise and use the power we have. Awareness, also, of our times of strength and our particular areas of strength can help to support us in more difficult times. This is using your own resources.

Some ways to boost your strength to maximum levels:

- Remind yourself that your feelings are an important and valuable part of you. You do not have to apologise for them. They are what makes you human.

- Remember that for bullies to exist, there have to be people who are prepared to be victims. Keep this in mind and refuse to allow yourself to be bullied by anyone. If you keep in mind that anyone who stands up to a bully is making the world a safer place for everyone, especially children, it will bring a new steel to your resolve. The subject of bullying at work is now openly acknowledged, discussed and condemned. If you need help on this one, ask for it.

- Identify the situations that you find most difficult to deal with powerfully. Rehearse what you might say and how you might act next time. The choice of language is vital in conveying strength. Work out ways of expressing yourself which put you in control. Practise role-playing these situations with a supportive friend.

- The best way of building up your strength is to remind yourself of what you've already coped with in your life and what you still want to achieve. The strong belief that you are a unique individual who has an important life to lead that no-one else in history can lead for you is the greatest way of giving you all the strength you need.

> *For me the greatest strength is the ability to be absolutely myself. This has taken years to learn, and it still requires the courage of my convictions and belief in my values. If I can be truly myself, it creates a light that spreads to others, encouraging them to do the same.*
>
> Lisa, UK

10. Enjoying it all!

That's the subject of the next chapter............

Life is the moment – why not seize it?

Chapter Seven
Enjoying the Ride

'Freedom....means knowing who you are, what you are supposed to be doing on this earth, and then simply doing it.'

Natalie Goldberg

And, we would add, "enjoying it". You've made the decision to become the person you want to be and have started changing your life to reflect this. You've chosen your vehicle and leapt into the seat – now let's make sure you have an exhilarating, amazing journey.

Feel the wind in your hair and relish the beautiful scenery! Yes, you do need to look where you're going, but don't fix your eyes so firmly on your goal that you miss what's around you on the journey.

As John Lennon said, life is what happens to you when you're busy making other plans.

Right at this moment, you have an incredible gift – the chance to live your life. You can compare your gift to everyone else's, but no-one else has anything like yours. No matter what you may have been through already, no matter what you dream for your future, the all-important thing is to enjoy the ride.

- **Enjoy your surroundings**

Without spending a fortune, you can make your living space beautiful. Decorate it the way you want, not how you think it 'should' be.

A good way to achieve this is to put away everything decorative – pictures, ornaments, photos – from a room. Then after a few days, bring back only those things that you really miss. These are the items that genuinely express your personal style.

Ensure that you have some contact with the natural world every day. Go outside and take time to notice and enjoy small things – flowers, birdsong, the breeze. It may sound old-fashioned, but taking pleasure in natural things is a great way to nourish your spirit – and it's free.

If you live in the country, you probably know all this already. If you live in a city, find a park or garden where you can walk in your lunchtime or in the evenings. Notice other people's gardens, window boxes, hanging baskets – instead of rushing past, take time to look and cherish them.

" *I create opportunities to get energy back: from the sunshine, an unbroken day in the grass, feeling the warmth on my skin and enjoying the colours of nature. This gives me all I need.* **"**

Karin Blauensteiner, Springboard Trainer, Austria

- **Enjoy your possessions**

You already have all that you need. It's difficult to believe this in our consumer-led and advert-driven society, but if you simplify enough, you'll find that you actually *need* very little. You may *want* more, but you don't *need* more.

If there is something material you want, pause to consider <u>why</u> you want it. Is it because someone else has it? Because you think others will admire you more if you have it? If you are able to be honest you may be surprised at your own answers.

Most of the items we buy do little more than take up space. Then we realise we didn't need them – and we throw them away, give them away or sell them on.

By wanting and needing less, you'll find you have more than enough. When people feel fulfilled, they overflow. When we overflow, we can easily afford to give some away – energy, money or happiness. If we are not fully satisfied ourselves, we find it very hard to be generous.

- **Enjoy who you are**

Blow your own trumpet, especially to yourself. You are a unique person, so be proud of it!

You may have heard of, or even use, 'affirmations'. An affirmation is a powerful, positive statement in the present tense. Some examples are:

> "I am OK just as I am."
> "Everything I need is already within me."
> "Whatever happens, I can handle it."
> "I am calm, strong and full of energy"

They are most effective when repeated daily to yourself, out loud.

NOTEBOOK

BE THE GREAT 'I AM'

What aspects of yourself are you using, building on and developing?

Translate this into a great 'I am' statement:
- I am energetic
- I am confident
- I am feeling calm
- I am successful
- I am growing

Think of as many as you can, then note them down. Remember, some of these may be what you are now, others are what you want to be – but keep them all in the present tense.

Say these statements aloud to yourself, whether it's in the bath, in the car, even walking along. This is not the time to be modest – be positive, proud and daring!

Write each affirmation on a separate card, keep them by your bedside and pick one at random when you wake up. Take the card with you and look at it from time to time during the day.

Add to your cards when you wish to, change the statements to suit you, but keep them positive, personal and in the present tense.

• **Enjoy 'Now'**

Although we spend a great deal of our time thinking about them, we can't actually *experience* the past or the future. We can only experience the present. **Now** is all we actually have to live in. It follows that we need to make our Now as perfect as we can – and we do this by finding the joy in what we have, and in where we are heading.

Go with the flow, take time, slow down. We need to find a balance between activity and relaxation.

> *I have started to value myself more and I now tell myself that I can do things if I want to. Every morning I look in the mirror and say to myself: "You're going to have a good day, so go out there and do it!"*
>
> Claire, Liverpool

We are human beings, not human doings.

Attachment to goals and achievements is necessary for progress, but detachment is also vital for our spiritual well-being.

The best combination for success is thought, action and reflection – without time to relax and reflect, how are we to learn from our actions or build up the energy for more activity?

" *How beautiful it is to do nothing and then rest afterwards.* **"**

Spanish proverb

Next time you are stuck in traffic or waiting in a queue, take a really deep breath. Don't fret about the delay. This is an ideal time to say some of the 'Great I am' statements, or to think what you can do to be different today.

Consider these as bonus moments to relax and reflect.

> **"** *I have never regretted the decision to become self-employed and cannot now imagine going back to working for an employer, though I have to admit to moments of acute tension when looking at the minimal bank balance! I have found that work invariably comes in just when I begin to wonder how I am going to pay the bills. Trust and believe in yourself is the name of the game!* **"**

Pam Day, Springboard Trainer, UK

- **Enjoy your creativity**

Never allow yourself to say, "I'm not creative." Believe you are creative – everyone is or has the potential to be. It is part of being human, not the preserve of an artistic or talented few.

Many experts believe that stifling creativity and turning a deaf ear to our creative impulses can lead to illness and depression. Allowing our creativity free rein makes our lives better and more fulfilling. So how can we make this happen?

Six Steps to Creativity

1. Try new experiences.

Do something different or go somewhere you've never been before. Make a point of doing at least one thing every day that takes you out of your usual comfort zone.

It doesn't have to cost money to try something new. It just takes some thought and effort.

Browse through the library, visit an art gallery, go to an auction or a jumble sale, wander round a garden centre, try on hats in a store, spend some time in a church, browse in a bookshop, even try reading a book or magazine on a subject you know nothing about. Do this alone and with an open mind. Just look, absorb, reflect.

2. Prepare your creative space and your supplies.

Find somewhere in your home where you can experiment with your creative skills. Get back in touch with what you most enjoyed when you were a child. Most children just love a box of 'stuff' to make things with.

What did you spend your pocket money on when you were little? So have fun, put together your own 'play box'. Be selfish and keep it just for you – don't try to share it with children!

Take time to enjoy collecting things for your box – coloured paper, ribbons, sequins, glue, felt tip pens, stickers, paints, modelling clay, wool, thread, scraps of fabric... The list is endless.

If your passions lie in the kitchen or the garden, collect accordingly. Browse through cookery books or gardening magazines and store up some special ingredients, seeds or bulbs. None of these need cost a fortune, especially if you browse first and choose the best value for money. That's part of the pleasure!

3. Give yourself time.

You'll need at least a couple of hours' solitude a week for your visits and your collecting excursions. Make sure you get the time! Practise having creative time to yourself and make it an unbreakable habit. If you have to do some prior planning, then do it and make it work for you. Use spare chunks of time, like waiting in the car or in the surgery. Have a notebook for jotting down ideas or a personal stereo with interesting tapes or a new kind of music.

4. Get started – just go ahead and DO IT!

Don't wait for the perfect moment, it won't arrive. Draw, paint, write poems, stories or songs, model with clay, sew, embroider, cook, sow seeds. You don't have to aim at a particular result. Just enjoy yourself. It's the doing that's important. The joy of creating is letting yourself go and becoming wholly absorbed in the process.

5. Guard our creativity.

If you're sensitive to other people's opinions, don't tell them what you're doing or show them the results. They won't necessarily understand what you're trying to achieve (maybe nothing except having a good time!) but they may feel obliged to comment or judge. Most people can't help themselves! If you're not worried about their possible reactions, show them your efforts or share your ideas. They may have something useful to contribute, or be inspired by you.

6. Collect ideas so you can keep going!

Get an index box or a file and make it your Ideas Box. It's sometimes known as a 'tickler' because when you're short on inspiration, something in the box may tickle your fancy.

Cut out articles from papers or magazines, jot down things people say or do, write down ideas that come to you when you haven't got time to pursue them.

If your creative energy begins to flag, think about asking a friend who may be interested in doing things together. Collect brochures from colleges and see if there's something that appeals to you – maybe a one-day workshop or an evening class. Look in your local paper or supermarket noticeboards for clubs or societies to join.

You don't have to stick with what you know – branch out and try something new.

Keeping the Fun and Enjoyment

How would you describe 'having fun' or 'enjoying yourself'? What thoughts come to mind?

It may be that you think of being with friends, family or being a child, it may be that you think of being alone and free to do whatever you please!

We know that 'All work and no play makes Jill a dull girl' – each of us needs a sense of 'play' and enjoyment, having fun alongside our work.

- Find ways to lift your spirits that require nothing other than thinking

- Find activities that you enjoy so that you can plan them in as part of your life

- Appreciate the people you care about and who make your life more joyful

Life does not have to be about denying yourself the things you enjoy, or just doing enough to 'get by'. Even when finances are short, there are ways to enjoy the ride.

Thankful Pages

You may want to use some pages in your notebook to make regular notes of things that you have experienced that have made you feel 'thankful'.

Examples might be:

getting a new job; changing your hairstyle; spending time in the countryside; feeling the wind in my hair;
or:
someone held the door open for me; the car started first time; an amazing sunset that I was able to see; a great song I haven't heard in years; watching a father cuddle his children.

In this way you can capture all the good things in life, from small, personal experiences to big changes – anything that gives you a warm glow and makes you feel grateful in some way.

What things have happened today that you are thankful about?

Keep loving and laughing and you can survive anything. Find the focus, work hard, get people to help you, believe in yourself, your ideas and abilities - and the possibilities are endless.

Terri, Australia

A Few Happy Thoughts!

All too often we focus on the negative. How about those moments that really lift your day?

What makes you laugh?
- Good comedies
- Being with my best friends
- Sharing fun memories with my family

What makes you feel content?
- Snuggling up on my own sofa with a good film
- A warm house
- A full tank of petrol and not having to be anywhere particular
- Going to bed without any worries on my mind

What do you treat yourself to?
- A lie-in on a Sunday, reading the newspapers
- The best quality coffee I can afford
- A take-away once a month
- Membership of the health club

What makes you feel alive?
- Enjoying the taste and texture of different foods
- A walk in the rain when I'm all wrapped-up
- Feeling the sun on my skin or sand between my toes
- Singing loudly to my favourite music when no-one else is around
- Doing something that's 'not me', even if I never do it again!

NOTEBOOK

YOUR HAPPY THOUGHTS

Write down as many as you can think of, whether they are actions, thoughts, memories or plans, with others or alone – the more you can capture, the better. Leave some space for other happy thoughts that you may want to add later.

Once you have a list of happy thoughts, you can draw on them if things are not going so well – they can act as an instant recipe book for things to think of or do that will lift you when you need it. They will also encourage you to keep thinking about whether you have work and play in balance while you are on your journey.

Quick positive pointers

1. Time for yourself
This is not an optional extra, it's essential. In just the same way as you might have to find time to go to work, feed the dog, do the shopping, you find time for yourself.

When we are under pressure, this is often the first to drop, because it seems non-essential, or it seems as though it doesn't affect anyone else. Yet if you miss out on doing the things that make you feel good, comforted, happy, exhilarated, it <u>does</u> affect the people around you, because you won't be feeling as positive or supportive as you could be.

Find time to do things for no other reason than 'I want to'. It's guaranteed that these times are worth the effort – you will reap the benefits, and others will be dealing with a more contented, positive you.

2. Resources are ongoing

The resources offered in this book are not only there to start you off. The best way to get the most from resources is to draw on them whenever you need them. It is a strength to be able to identify resources and support and to use them effectively.

3. What is your buzz?

Identify what it is about your life that really gives you a 'buzz'. Is it that you are achieving something you have wanted for a long time? Is it that you are developing your talents? Trying new things? Helping others? Doing something different?

Whatever is at the heart of what you are living for, hold onto that and make it one of your happy thoughts.

Remember you have worth as an individual and you have the opportunity to be successful and happy. You do have to work at it, you do have to keep an open and receptive mind, you do have to have a go, be prepared for setbacks and remember your life is what you make it.

Julia, Australia

4. Do something positive for someone else

If you want to feel great, do something great for someone else – far from taking away your energy, it can give you energy. Whether you take a bag of your 'cast offs' to a charity shop, photocopy a piece of work that a colleague is interested in, cook a special meal for your partner or send a note to an old friend – spread a bit of joy around.

Seeing someone else smile might be all the inspiration you need.

CHAPTER 8
The Vision

'The future belongs to those who believe in the beauty of their dreams.'

Eleanor Roosevelt

The word 'vision' is often used in connection with the future and with imagination.

A true vision is even more about the present - how you perceive and act on what's happening in the world today. For example, women have made much progress in their struggle for equality, and this has only happened through individuals acting on their vision and making it real.

The *Springing Forward* vision is one of a world where everyone is treated and valued equally and everyone has the opportunity to fulfil their potential in whatever way they want.

How can I influence the future?

More and more people are articulating their visions and working towards them. If you want to join them, give yourself time to work on your vision – it's not something you can just snatch out of the air. It takes thought and feeling.

Whether you intend to or not, you will automatically influence the future in some way – so you can choose to influence it positively. You may find that a particular event or trend within your experience intrigues and interests you. Think about it and see where it might go in the future.

If you have always felt strongly about the unfair treatment of people in low-paid jobs, you can join a campaign group; you can find out about what other people are doing and add to their strength. If there is no such group – there is always the choice to start one yourself.

If you feel strongly about how few women there are in positions of authority, find out about groups acting to change this –Δ search on the Internet, look in the library, read the papers. Focus on what you feel and what you want to change, then find a way of contributing to that change.

Affecting others locally

Are you the kind of person about whom others say, 'She's great, isn't she, always looks for the best in people'?

We all talk about other people, and they will always talk about us. Imagine that every bad thing you say about a person sticks to her somehow, like an invisible piece of mud weighing her down. That person doesn't know you ever said anything, she never heard it, but the very fact it was said somehow clings to her.

What about if something positive were said instead? Imagine that for every positive thing you ever say about someone, it somehow adds an invisible glow to her that will always stay with her.

Of course, you cannot expect to be nice to everyone all the time, and you can't expect them to always be nice to you. But how many times have you said something negative or unkind about someone that really didn't need to be said?

If everyone managed to say fewer unkind things about others, imagine how much bad feeling that would take out of the world.

Affecting others globally

Some people focus on one burning ambition –

- Anita Roddick and her determination to have environmentally-friendly cosmetics

- Mother Teresa and her dedication to helping others

- Trevor Bayliss and his invention of a wind-up radio for use in third world countries

There are many more people who have also had a worldwide impact but without gaining the same recognition. Many of them do not realise how much they affected others – Mozart, whose gift for music has brought joy to millions, died in poverty, unaware that his music would last for so many generations.

Even a single idea, a piece of writing, a picture, a saying, a gift that you have within you can reach unknown people throughout the world. Sounds impossible? How do you know unless you have tried? Remember the power of the Net!

V•I•S•I•O•N

VOCATION

The word 'vocation' literally means 'calling'. Jobs that need a particular type of person and a special sort of dedication are referred to as 'callings', like being a priest or a nun. This somehow implies that other jobs are of a lower or lesser degree. There is no reason to believe this.

Finding and doing the work that only you were born to do is just as much of a vocation, whether this is by becoming a nun, a nurse, or by answering telephones or cleaning offices.

This is the start of my 19th year in the public service. I worked in the Education Department for the first seven years, first as a Laboratory Assistant and then as the Secretary to a Primary School. I transferred from the Primary school to the Chiders Court House, and once I started work there, I knew I had found my true niche in life.

Kerryn, Australia

People often express their sense of a 'vocation' by saying, 'I know that there is something I am supposed to do with my life, but I haven't found it yet...' or 'I need to find my niche in life, then I can really spread my wings'.

Make the most of you!

Whoever you are, you are absolutely unique with your own strengths, talents, abilities and potential. You have an enormous amount to give to the world, whether that is literally worldwide, or simply to those who know you.

Make the most of all your talents and your gifts, your special abilities and your potential. Remember that no-one else quite has the gifts that you do, and that human beings appreciate sharing and enjoying other people's gifts and talents.

You may not be a singer, but you may love to hear someone singing; you may not be an artist but you love to enjoy other people's work; you may be hopeless at DIY and practical things, but you love to see furniture that is beautifully crafted. So, whatever your gifts are, be thankful for them, and find ways to share them with others.

We can't all have every gift or ability, but if we share them, everyone can have access to them and enjoy it.

NOTEBOOK

GIFTS GALORE

Note down the qualities and gifts that you admire in others and that you share in or experience. How do you feel when you can share or enjoy someone else's gift?

Spend some minutes thinking about your own abilities and gifts – not comparing them to how well someone else does this or that, but just what you feel are your gifts. Note down your strengths and talents.

How do you feel when you acknowledge and appreciate your own gifts?

INTUITION

Most of us spend our lives listening to the voices of others. We listen to the voices of our parents, our siblings, our older relations, our teachers, our school friends, our colleagues, our managers. There are so many voices in our ears that the noise blocks out the quieter voice of our own intuition.

We are often taught to pay attention to the voices outside us but very seldom asked to take note of the whispering <u>inside</u>.

> *I see my personal development as very much ongoing, and I hope I never reach the stage where I feel I have nothing more to learn about myself.*
>
> Jan, UK

Of course there is much good advice on offer from other people. It would be foolish – and dangerous – to go through life ignoring what others tell us. But that is only part of the story.

To live out our vision, we need to discriminate between what others want of us and what we want for ourselves. It is generally expected of women that they be sensible and compliant. Perhaps that's why it's taking time for women to make a difference to the world we live in. We need to become <u>more</u> headstrong, not less.

We will never truly find the work we were born to do until we learn to listen to ourselves and trust what we hear.

SERENITY

The 20th Century saw an incredible change of pace in the western world. The number of things that can be achieved in a single day is just amazing, and with technological advances, the speed is set to carry on increasing.

Sometimes, it is hard to realise that we do not have to live at this frenetic pace. It may be that your job or your home life requires a lot of you each day, but even so...

- allow yourself times when you can simply sit back for a while and let the world carry on around you
- give yourself moments when you can take it easy
- grant yourself indulgences that help you to feel calm and relaxed
- create days when you do not care what time it is

And through your everyday life, no matter how busy you are, try to find a sense of serenity that you hold on to.

In this sense, serenity is peace of mind, knowing what 'enough' means, and feeling secure from within. Be aware of what *really* matters to you, aside from the belongings, the bank balance, or getting everywhere on time. Find ways to enjoy who you are and what you have – and let that be enough.

Learn to accept that you cannot be all things to all people – but you can be yourself.

"
How many cares one loses when one decides to be
not something but someone.
"

Coco Chanel

Inspiration

Find inspiration – look for people who have a vision, talk about it and act on it. Perhaps you don't know many people like this yet, but they can be found.

When your vision for yourself becomes clear, seek out others who have similar interests and values. Get involved with them in projects that are designed to move things forward. As you spend more time with them, your own vision will be strengthened and enhanced.

Become inspirational – if you act as if your vision were already true, you will be instrumental in making it come true. In this way, being a visionary is a way of living *now*, not just a hope for the future.

A few years from now...

Imagine you are watching a TV programme or listening to the radio. There's an interview with one of the most successful women in the world. She's telling the interviewer that the one thing that convinced her to pursue her dream was a woman she knew who had a really positive outlook on life, who didn't just dream but made her dreams reality and encouraged others to do the same.

Imagine she names you.

That is what real inspiration means. You don't need to be famous or in a senior position to be an inspiration to others. When asked about the most influential person in her life, many successful women mention someone unknown to most of us but particularly meaningful to them.

Pirkko Pölönen, Springboard Trainer, Finland

I have been renovating my house, and it reflects how I have been rebuilding my life. On the change of the millennium, I became fifty years old. This span of years has taken me through different turns, big and small changes. Sometimes I wonder what will happen next. This curiosity gives me strength when others try to slow me down, or try to find reasons why I should forget my latest plans and dreams.

I have severe hearing and vision impairments, and they give colour to my personality. My mind is always questioning. What is the position of a disabled woman in a relationship, in a family, in society? How can disabled women, such a minority, survive in society? Many times, I have been asked, 'Pirkko, where do you find your amazing strength?'

I am sure that what I have is an adult woman's 'super-strength', coupled with the ability to be humble when appropriate, and curiosity about the special things that life can offer. The energy of womanhood gives me the joy of life and strength. It will carry me through life, if I trust in it and do something about it.

You will also have the 'super-strength' if you just keep looking and listening for it!

Every day you are influencing and affecting others around you – your family, your friends, even people you pass on the street. Even with a smile or a frown, you are shaping the future. We are all making a difference to the world and creating the history that others will be born into.

ONENESS

Every single thing in the world is connected to everything else – nothing happens without a reaction. This is known in scientific circles as 'chaos theory'.

So interconnected is life around the world that, in theory at least, the tiniest change in air pressure in one part of the globe could affect the weather on an entirely different continent.

This is how a butterfly beating its wings in a tropical rainforest could potentially trigger a cyclone in the United States.

Although each of us is an individual, we are related in some way to all other life on the planet. We share our space and lives with all the diverse elements in the world, the variety of people and all living things.

> *Self-growth and all-round development of women is truly crucial to become positive, responsible and committed human beings, particularly as women remain, and will remain, the pillars of all sections of society.*
>
> Ms Prema Viswanathan, India

Through all our differences we are part of an amazing whole. You can connect with and affect an unknown number of people with your actions and the way you choose to live your life.

No going back!

Once you've started on this journey to become your real self, there is no retreat. Life becomes a great and glorious adventure.

You may find that your vision changes as you grow and develop. Let it. To have one fixed, immutable vision is to limit yourself and stunt your growth.

You'll know when you're living your vision because you'll no longer have to keep checking how you're doing or how far you've got. It will simply be part of who you are and what you stand for.

"

No other woman on earth can do what you alone are called to do, can give to the world what you alone were sent to give through your authentic gifts. The call may be so faint you can barely make out the message, but if you listen, you will *hear it.* **"**

Sarah Ban Breathnach

What is Springboard?

Springboard is an award-winning women's development programme. The overall aim is to enable women to decide on the next steps for their development and equip them with the positive attitude and skills to take those steps. Springboard is usually run within organisations but occasionally there are also public programmes, which any woman may attend. All programmes are delivered by Springboard trainers who are specially chosen, trained and licensed by The Springboard Consultancy.

The programme consists of workshops, a workbook, practical role models and networking. The workbook is available to any woman, from good bookshops or from Hawthorn Press. Topics covered include dealing with change, goal-setting, assertiveness, balancing work and home, finding support, building contacts and putting yourself across positively.

In the last ten years, Springboard has spread to 14 countries and has reached over 120,000 women. Many of these women and their trainers are featured in the book and all the women quoted are 'real people' and the quotes are their exact words.

Getting in Touch

If you would like to know more about the Springboard programme, please contact:

The Springboard Consultancy
Holwell
East Down
Barnstaple
Devon EX31 4NZ

Tel: +44 (0) 1271 850828
Fax: +44 (0) 1271 850130

Email: office@springboardconsultancy.com
Website: www.springboardconsultancy.com

Other Books From Hawthorn Press

Springboard
Liz Willis and Jenny Daisley

Springboard helps you do what you want to do in your life and work. It gives you the ideas and skills to take more control of your life and then gives you the boost in self confidence to start making things happen. *Springboard* is for all women at work; whether you are in full time or part time employment, considering employment, wanting to return to work, just starting out, or approaching retirement - *Springboard* helps you to be the best you can be!

Springboard is a workbook packed with ideas, exercises and examples that you can either work through on your own, or with two or three others. t is down-to-earth, practical and full of positive thinking and good humour, with the points illustrated with cartoons and real case studies. This new edition is fully revised and updated. You can work through the workbook on its own or as part of the Springboard Women's Development Programme. Contents include; assertiveness; setting goals; what you've got going for you; finding support; the world about you; blowing your own trumpet; more energy - less anxiety; making things happen; your personal resource bank; balancing home and work; networking; useful addresses.

'*Springboard* was a turning point for me. It opened my eyes to my potential'. Katie Whichelow, *Campaign Manager, Opportunity Now*

'What is particularly impressive is that everyone on the course has reported personal progress. They are more assertive, more confident and more committed.' *Tarmac Plc*

5th edition; 320pp; 297 x 210mm; 1 869 890 10 8; paperback.

Navigator
Men's development workbook
James Traeger, Jenny Daisley and Liz Willis

Navigator is one of the very first personal and professional development workbooks in the UK specifically developed for all men at work, on their own or in relationships and as fathers and sons.

Life for men is changing, and changing fast. Many men are asking who they are and where they, and their expectations of life, fit in with these rapid changes. *Navigator* provides individual men with a down-to-earth way of tackling many of these issues.

Navigator forms the basis of a 3-month Men's Development Programme recently researched and piloted inside a wide range of UK organisations, including BT Mobile, Braintree District Council, Midland Bank, NatWest UK, Wolverhampton MBC, The University of Cambridge and The University of London.

Navigator is full of positive thinking and good humour and is packed with ideas, examples and practical exercises with the points illustrated with cartoons and real case studies.

Contents include:

* realistic self-assessment
* challenging expectations
* a man's world
* clarifying values
* taking risks and making changes
* physical and feelings fitness
* setting a goal strategy that works
* assertiveness for men
* putting yourself across

288pp; 297 x 210mm; 1 869 890 80 9; paperback.

Manhood

An action plan for changing men's lives
Steve Biddulph

Most men don't have a life. So begins the most powerful, practical and honest book ever to be written about men and boys. Not about our problems – but about how we can find the joy and energy of being in a male body with a man's mind and spirit – about men's liberation.

Steve Biddulph, author of Raising Boys and the million-seller The Secret of Happy Children, writes about the turning point that men have reached – as reflected in films like The Full Monty. He gives practical personal answers to how things can be different from the bedroom to the workplace. He tells powerful stories about healing the rift between fathers and sons. About friendship. How women and men can get along in dynamic harmonious ways. How boys can be raised to be healthy men.

Manhood has had a profound emotional impact on tens of thousands of readers worldwide, and has been passed from son to father, friend to friend, husband to wife, with the simple message 'you must read this!'

272pp; 216 x 138mm; 1 869 890 99 X; paperback.

'Steve Biddulph should be in the UK what he is in Australia, the household name in the business of raising boys and being a man.'
Dorothy Rowe, psychologist and writer

People in Charge
Creating self managing workplaces
Robert Rehm

Powerful and practical, Participative Design enables companies to create more productive workplaces and better results. Here are the tools for creating self managing workplaces using Participative Design. The concepts, do-it-yourself guide and helpful examples show how people can re-design their work. The result is a more productive workplace full of energy, learning, quality and pride. And people in charge of their work.

Participative Design was devised by Fred Emery in the 1970's. Here, Robert Rehm shows how managers and workers can use Participative Design to do a better job. And putting people in charge works. Examples include the US Federal Courts, a Prudential call centre, the South African Land Bank, retail stores, a wine company and the conductor-less Orpheus Orchestra of New York.

Contents: The self managing workplace; the six criteria for productive work; origins of Participative Design; the workshop; a start up guide for self managing teams; case studies; resources.

288pp; 243 x 189mm; 1 869 890 87 6; paperback.

Confronting Conflict
A first-aid kit for handling conflict
Friedrich Glasl

Conflict costs! When tensions and differences are ignored they grow into conflicts, injuring relationships, groups and organisations. So, how can we tackle conflict successfully? Dr Friedrich Glasl has worked with conflict resolution in companies, schools and communities for over 30 years, earning him and his techniques enormous respect. *Confronting Conflict* is authoritative and up to date, containing new examples, exercises theory and techniques.

Confronting Conflict will be useful for managers, facilitators, management lecturers and professionals such as teachers and community workers, mediators and workers in dispute resolution.

192pp; 216 x 138mm; 1 869 890 71 X; paperback

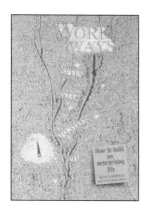

Workways: Seven Stars to Steer By
Biography workbook for building a more enterprising life
Kees Locher and Jos van der Brug

This biography workbook helps you consider your working life, and make more conscious choices, at a time of great change in our 'workways'. Background readings, thirty seven exercises and creative activities are carefully structured for individuals or self-help groups.

352pp; 297 x 210mm; 1 869 890 89 2; paperback.

Parenting Matters
Ways to bring up your children using heart and head
Parentline Plus

Parenting Matters helps you bring up loving and happy children. Here is the heart to becoming the more confident, sensitive relaxed, firm and caring parent that you truly are – enjoying your children and family.

Parenting Matters is a workbook packed with ideas, exercises and examples for personal use. It supports your learning on the course run by Parentline Plus. This sensible and positive approach has been successfully developed by parents for parents over many years.

228pp; 297 x 210mm; 1 869 890 16 7; paperback.

Being a Parent
Parentline Plus

Being a parent is one of the most important jobs in the world, because parents hold the future in their hands. Parents need all the help they can get. Yet many battle on without any support or guidance.

There are many different approaches to parenting. In our multi-cultural world, there is no one way of bringing up children that is right for everyone. *Being a Parent* helps you find out what works best for you and your children. This friendly and helpful book can be used on its own or as a workbook for the Parentline Plus course, Understanding Children 1, which is accredited by the National Open College Network.

96pp; 297 x 210mm; 1 869 890 81 7; paperback.